Blue Skies:

New thinking about the future of higher education

A collection of short articles by leading commentators

Edited by Louis Coiffait

Pearson Centre for Policy and Learning
www.pearsonblueskies.com

ALWAYS LEARNING

Blue Skies:

New thinking about the future of higher education

A collection of short articles by leading commentators

Contents

6

About the Pearson Centre for Policy and Learning

At a time of growing demand and enormous change in the world of education and skills, both nationally and globally, the Pearson Centre for Policy and Learning (PCPL) aims to harness the depth and breadth of expertise within Pearson (the world's leading learning company), and our partners, to provide a clear, positive and respected voice on the lomg-term education issues that matter. It does this through the provision of:

- a range of **research** activities, offering evidence-based and original thinking
- respected, timely and useful **policy analysis** through channels such as Policy Watch, Primary Policy Watch, Policy Tracker and Hot Breakfast Briefings
- engaging and enjoyable **events**, briefings and presentations that offer informed insight, in-depth analysis and measured debate
- high quality **publications** of value to both policymakers and practitioners
- **support to the wider Pearson business** through policy and research intelligence on external developments, as well as encouraging blue sky thinking

You can find more information about the Centre at www.pearsoncpl.com.

Acknowledgements

First and foremost we would like to thank each of the contributors for giving their time and expertise to this project. The diversity of the considered commentary expressed across the different articles in this collection provides both new thinking and real hope about the future of higher education.

The editor is also grateful to Pearson colleagues for their comments, support and advice.

The views expressed in this publication are those of the authors alone.

8

The authors

Mary Abdo is the Project Lead on the Citizens' University at the Young Foundation. Previously, Mary was the Practice Lead for Youth Transitions, with responsibility for The Youth of Today. Before that she was a consultant with McKinsey spin-off Portas Consulting and a Director at a Los Angeles literacy programme Reading to Kids. Mary has a Masters of Public Policy from Harvard.

Alison Allden is the Chief Executive of HESA, is a Fellow of the British Computer Society, sits on the JISC (Joint Information Systems Committee) Board and is also a member of the Information Standards Board.

Robert Anderson is Professor Emeritus of History at the University of Edinburgh. He has written extensively on the history of universities.

Libby Aston is Director of The University Alliance and has held previous roles at The Russell Group, the Parliamentary Select Committee for Education and Skills, the Higher Education Funding Council for England (HEFCE) and the Higher Education Policy Institute (HEPI).

Phil Baty is Editor of the Times Higher Education World University Rankings and Deputy Editor of the Times Higher Education magazine. The latest world university rankings results can be found here: http://bit.ly/thewur.

Bahram Bekhradnia is Director of HEPI, was formerly the Director of Policy at HEFCE for ten years and has advised twenty different national governments on the financing of higher education.

Sue Betts, the Director of Linking London, is an educationalist with a long and varied career. A former Vice Principal, she had responsibility for curriculum, staff development and higher education in the Further Education Sector. She has worked for a National Awarding Body, two national distributed e-learning organisations, and as a consultant. As Director, Sue is responsible for the strategic direction of Linking London.

Dame Lynne Brindley has been the Chief Executive of the British Library since 2000 and Chaired the 2009-11 HEFCE Online Learning Task Force.

Professor Sally Brown is Emeritus Professor at Leeds Metropolitan University where she was Pro-Vice-Chancellor (Academic), Adjunct professor at the University of the Sunshine Coast, Queensland and Visiting Professor at the University of Plymouth.

Dr Kate Burrell is an experienced project manager with a background in teaching, cell biology and neuroscience. More recently her work on partnership and business development in Linking London has included relationship building, brokering progression agreements as well as joint authoring a number of practical reports and publications.

Ezri Carlebach was Communications & Research Director at Lifelong Learning UK, the sector skills council for post-compulsory education employers, until it closed in March 2011. He has previously held senior marketing and communications roles in higher education, the arts and heritage sector and financial services. He now works on a number of strategic communications projects and is completing a Master's in Philosophy at Birkbeck College.

Caroline Chipperfield is Policy Advisor to the Vice-Chancellor at the University of Plymouth.

Paul Clark is Director of Policy at Universities UK where he is responsible for coordinating the organisation's full range of policy and research activity, working to influence national developments in higher education, and shaping the future policy agenda.

Louis Coiffait is a Policy Manager within the Pearson Centre for Policy and Learning where he is researching issues such as higher education, enterprise education, STEM skills, education data and careers advice. He tweets and blogs on higher education policy news and analysis at @LouisMMCoiffait and www.pearsoncpl.com/category/HE-policy-blog. Louis is also a Fellow of the RSA, a regular volunteer, a school Governor in Hackney and runs the social enterprise Work&Teach in his spare time.

Fathima Dada is the CEO of Pearson Southern Africa. She has worked on educational policies for the Ministry of Education for the past 11 years, and continues to do this and community development work, especially in rural areas of South Africa.

David Docherty is Chief Executive of the Council For Industry and Higher Education (CIHE), and Chairman of the Digital Television Group, which is the industry body for digital television in the UK.

Nick Davy is the Higher Education Policy Manager at the Association of Colleges (AoC).

Annie Gosling is the King George VI Fellow at Cumberland Lodge and a PhD student at Liverpool John Moores University. She is writing her thesis on young people's career aspirations and expectations.

Dr James Goulding is an early career researcher with a rapidly growing list of international publications across the fields of data theory, location based services, information retrieval and ubiquitous computing. Extremely experienced software engineer with a passion for Open and Linked data and an extensive range of programming skills, specialising in mobile technologies, distributed databases and artificial intelligence techniques.

Dr Owen Gower is a Senior Fellow at Cumberland Lodge and a Visiting Tutor in Philosophy at Royal Holloway and King's College London.

Dr Matt Grist is a Senior Researcher on the Family and Society Programme at Demos. His expert areas include education (including vocational education), capabilities, social mobility, youth policy and behaviour change.

Martin Hughes is a writer, specialising in higher education policy and the student experience. He blogs for students at TheUniversityBlog and can be found linking all sorts of HE material via Twitter at @universityboy.

Paul Jackson is the Chief Executive of EngineeringUK, a Chartered Engineer and Fellow of the Institution of Engineering and Technology.

Sam Jones is Head of Communications and Public Affairs at The University Alliance, with previous roles working for Vince Cable and Peter Mandelson at the Department for Business, Innovation and Skills and in the private sector, including with Harrods.

Professor James Ladyman is Professor of Philosophy at the University of Bristol and is Co-Editor of The British Journal for the Philosophy of Science.

Sir Alan Langlands is the Chief Executive of HEFCE. He was formerly the Principal and Vice-Chancellor of the University of Dundee (2000-2009) and Chief Executive of the National Health Service (NHS) in England (1994-2000).

Professor Craig Mahoney is Chief Executive of The Higher Education Academy, is a Chartered Psychologist and was past Chair of the British Association of Sport and Exercise Sciences (BASES).

Julia Margo is Deputy Director at Demos. Julia is a regular commentator in the international and national press. She also writes for national, online and specialist press and is an experienced chair and public speaker on a wide range of subjects.

Paul Marshall is Executive Director of The 1994 Group. He is responsible for the management of all Group activity including policy development, government liaison and stakeholder relations. He is also a member of the UCAS Qualification Information Review Reference Group, CMI Academy Employer Board and the Research Concordat Executive Group.

Professor Derek McAuley is Professor of Digital Economy in the School of Computer Science and Director of Horizon, a Digital Economy Research Institute, at the University of Nottingham, and Affiliated Lecturer at the University of Cambridge Computer Laboratory. He is a Fellow of the British Computer Society and member of the UKCRC, a computing research expert panel of the IET and BCS.

Julie Mercer is a Partner in Deloitte's consulting practice and leads the education services practice.

Geoff Mulgan is currently the Chief Executive of the Young Foundation and will become the new Chief Executive of NESTA in June 2011. Some of his previous roles include; Director of Tony Blair's Strategy Unit, Founder and Director of the think-tank Demos, Chief Adviser to Gordon Brown MP, a lecturer in telecommunications, an investment executive, and a reporter on BBC TV and radio. He is a visiting professor at LSE, UCL and Melbourne University.

Jamie O'Connell is Marketing Director of The Student Room and is responsible for organisation strategy, ensuring the website offers the best possible service and functionality for all students and universities. He feels passionately about the role peer to peer support can play in education.

Gareth Parry is Professor of Education and Director of the Centre for the Study of Higher Education and Lifelong Learning at the University of Sheffield.

Nick Pearce is Director of IPPR, the Institute for Public Policy Research.

Dr Wendy Piatt is Director General of The Russell Group. She was previously Deputy Director and head of public service reform at the Prime Minister's Strategy Unit where she has also led work on social mobility, education and skills, local government and digital inclusion. Prior to that, she was Head of Education Policy at the Institute for Public Policy Research, specialising in higher and further education.

Aaron Porter is the National President of the NUS, serving from 10 June 2010 to 01 July 2011. Previously he was twice elected as the NUS Vice-President (Higher Education) and took leading roles in the University of Leicester Students' Union.

Professor Wendy Purcell is Vice-Chancellor at the University of Plymouth.

Professor Phil Race is Visiting Professor at the University of Plymouth, and Emeritus Professor of Leeds Metropolitan University. He publishes widely on teaching, learning and assessment. More information can be found on his website at www.phil-race. co.uk.

Dr Hanif Rahemtulla is Geospatial Scientist at the University of Nottingham and External Lecturer and Honorary Fellow at University College London. His research is principally focused in the areas of geographic information policy focusing on Open and Linked Data, the handling and analysis of environmental information, and wider philosophical issues on the societal impacts of Information Communication Technologies.

Peter Rawling is Deputy Head of The Windsor Boys School and for over thirty years has co-ordinated the Higher Education work there. Since 2007 he has chaired the Partnership's Higher Education group.

Johnny Rich is a media and higher education specialist with various roles as Publisher of brands such as Push (the leading independent resource for prospective students), Real World Magazine, the Recruiters' Guide to Courses & Campuses and the Oxbridge Students' Careers Resource. He is also a director of the Higher Education Academy. He appears regularly on television and radio as a specialist on students and higher education issues.

Charles Seaford is Head of the Centre for Well-being at nef (the new economics foundation) and takes an overview role of all of its work. He is a member of the ONS Advisory Forum on national well-being and was the author of nef's recent report on the economics of housing, One Million Homes.

Dr Catherine Such is Head of Research and Higher Education at the Royal Geographical Society (with the Institute of British Geographers). Previously, she was Professor of Geography at Indiana University, USA.

Stefan Stern is a former FT columnist, is now Visiting Professor at Cass Business School, London, and Director of Strategy at Edelman, the PR firm. He has two noisy but highly teachable children.

Laura Stoll is an Assistant Researcher at the Centre for Well-being at nef. She has been researching for the History of Wellbeing project and co-ordinates the All-Party Parliamentary Group on Wellbeing Economics.

Pam Tatlow is Chief Executive of the university think-tank, million+ and has worked at a senior level in education, health and public affairs.

David Willetts is the UK Minister for Universities and Science.

Professor Geoff Whitty is Director Emeritus at the Institute of Education, University of London.

Foreword

Rod Bristow

Many of the most exciting, challenging and innovative ideas in human history have either been developed in or improved by universities – creating brilliant thinkers and helping to change the world around us.

These days more students than ever before want degree level education. Despite pressures on funding and access, I predict that the growth in participation in higher education will be relentless; young people will demand it, because employers will demand it. But there will surely be changes in the nature of the higher education that students want. I'm not just talking about the 'student experience'. Given the focus on employment most students have these days, the degrees they'll value most are the ones that equip best for the real world of work. That's not to say education will inevitably become depressingly utilitarian in its nature. Education should always be about the world at large too. But perhaps, the world of work and the world at large, are becoming more and more similar.

At Pearson we have a long history publishing in higher education. Today we are helping to educate over 100 million people in over 60 countries, many of them in higher education. In the future we will keep developing great content and services that engage learners and support lecturers; we will make our products even more user-friendly; we'll invest more in digital and online technologies; we'll make better use of data to personalise learning; and we'll do all this in partnership with universities across the sector.

We're not in higher education for the short-term. We take the long-term view. That's why we are supporting this collection of essays from the Pearson Centre for Policy and Learning, providing a platform for new ideas and debate.

Like many higher education colleagues, I see several global and national trends converging, resulting in an inflection point, where decisions made now will have a major impact on the future. Higher education will respond to these changes as it always has, innovating and adapting to make the most of opportunities and address the challenges. This won't be an easy process; the way ahead is unclear and those who seem certain of the answers should perhaps be cautious, and read this book. I hope that you enjoy it. Please let us know what you think about it and the issues it raises.

Rod Bristow is the President of Pearson UK, with a background in education and publishing.

Introduction

Louis Coiffait

Background and purpose of Blue Skies

This publication was first proposed in late 2010, at a moment when higher education (HE), particularly but not only in the UK, seemed to be entering a period of dramatic change. Many of those who study the history of higher education; have worked in the field for years; or have an international perspective appeared to agree that what was starting to happen in the UK held great significance. Lord Browne had just published his report on funding, recommending an unprecedented increase in tuition fees (to among the highest in the OECD), which the relatively new Coalition Government had largely accepted and outraged students had started protesting over. The lucrative flow of international students also looked at risk as a new immigration cap was posited. Meanwhile, the wider UK economy was still sluggishly recovering from the financial crisis, with the Comprehensive Spending Review laying out a bleak picture of major budget cuts, especially to the HE teaching budget (taking it to among the lowest in the OECD), especially in arts and humanities subjects.

This major reduction in public funding was supposed to be filled by private funding sources (primarily individual learners, via loans), and a more commercial system encouraged, with money following learners, demand shaping provision and new players entering the market. Furthermore, this all took place within an international context that featured an increasingly global marketplace for HE; growing diversity of provision; new delivery models, changing student expectations, fickle financial forces and rapid technological change. Some seemed to feel that the UK's HE system, a long-established jewel in the UK's economic, social and cultural crown, was under threat of radical change from many different quarters at once.

However you might feel about the true severity of this situation, the likely causes, or the best solutions: it is happening. At the time of writing, as we see each UK institution declaring its tuition fees (usually above the estimated £7,500 average), we are awaiting a delayed higher education White Paper, that will probably have to address that more-costly-than-anticipated demand in some way.

In this context it would have been wrong to undertake a piece of lengthy, rigorous research. Such work would report back too late to be truly useful and probably address the wrong issues. Now is the time for an open debate and new thinking from those who are best-placed to comment. This book is intended to provide a non-partisan platform for that debate, presenting a wide range of different opinions about the issues and priorities that matter to the future of higher education, in the UK and beyond.

There is (at times considerable) disagreement about priorities and methods, but common themes do seem evident. Most of our contributors are people and organisations you might expect to think wisely on the future of HE – but some are less well known or well heard, but equally well placed to comment. Blue Skies is a deliberate attempt to broaden the conversation fundamentally, completely re-framing some issues, and to propose a few bold and innovative solutions. By focussing on the future this book forces attention upon the crucial 'so what' questions.

Above all, this book aims to paint a positive picture for the future of higher education. It draws out the many strengths within the sector, showcases some of the best thinking available, demonstrates the breadth, passion and expertise of the authors, and hopefully provides some hope for the future.

Approach

This publication involves a targeted call for contributions, working with leading thinkers in the field to invite short, focussed articles under the 'big-tent' idea of 'new thinking about the future of higher education'. Editorial influence has been kept to the bare minimum. Views from a few key individuals within Pearson are included but have been given no special emphasis over others.

A note on language

Higher education, HE, HEIs, universities, the academy, tertiary education, academia, higher-level learning, Level Six – call it what you will, in most non-technical uses, these words mean the same thing to the majority of people. Often those using them don't even appreciate the subtle differences between the different words. The etymology of the word 'university' reveals its heritage in the classical Greek concept of a 'universal' education, covering a broad array of what we would now call subjects, and often including different types of learning. The word then became more formalised as a type of organisational structure; a corporation, community or association of students, teachers and researchers. More recently, the concept has been broadened further beyond *what* is studied *where,* to *who* is studying, as demonstrated by modern pre-occupations of moving higher education from an elite to a universal service, widening access and driving social mobility. However the issue of language is not a trivial one, for as many of the articles within this collection show, the sometimes simplistic and anachronistic concepts and assumptions used when considering higher education deserve to be challenged at times because they can limit both our understanding and the future opportunities available.

How to read Blue Skies

Blue Skies can be read in a number of ways. Cover-to-cover it provides a diverse and thought-provoking tour around all of the major challenges and opportunities facing the sector. Alternatively the reader can focus on the individual authors and article topics of interest. The sections attempt to group the articles in line with their main focus. However cross-cutting themes such as globalisation, technology and access run through many of the articles.

The hard copy of the book is also accompanied by a website (http://blueskies. pearson.com) which features summary videos from the authors as well as all of the book content in an online format, including downloadable PDFs. Readers are encouraged to visit the site, view the videos, share the content and add their own comments. Although this publication is very much 'of the moment' it is intended to provide lasting value in the future as a reference point at a time of major change.

Section one – Will the finances work?

Putting students at the heart of higher education

David Willetts

The UK Coalition Government immediately accepted the main thrust of Lord Browne's independent review of higher education, when it was published last year, because it put students at the heart of a more dynamic system. In all the controversy surrounding the parliamentary votes, the student demonstrations and the raw politics, this has been forgotten too often.

The review team had a clear overarching objective:

"we are relying on student choice to drive up quality. Students will control a much larger proportion of the investment in higher education. They will decide where the funding should go; and institutions will compete to get it. As students will be paying more than in the current system, they will demand more in return."

This key concept was not plucked from thin air. Half a century ago, it was a feature of the Robbins report, which called for higher fees so that universities' incomes were more closely linked to the students they taught. In the event, policy went in the opposite direction and university fees for home students disappeared from view.

But, as Lord Robbins himself said, the idea of a graduate contribution was "ultimately very difficult to resist." So, in 1997, the Dearing report recommended graduates should contribute one-quarter of the average cost of tuition via new income-contingent loans. After another false start, during which the first Blair Government introduced upfront fees, tuition loans were finally implemented in 2006.

Despite being couched in the language of consumer power, the settlement turned out to be the archetypal New Labour compromise: expensive to the taxpayer and unresponsive to the user. That is why the Browne report marked such an important shift. Using the same logic as Robbins and Dearing before him, Lord Browne called for far more of the teaching costs to be covered by a progressive loans system. If the taxpayer contributions were to shift substantially away from upfront institutional teaching grants towards loans put in the hands of students, then the system could finally become truly responsive. To lubricate the system, it would also be necessary to ensure better information for prospective students, to relax student number controls at an institutional level and to welcome new, quality higher education providers.

One of the key benefits of a more responsive system should be a greater emphasis on teaching quality. In the numerous university visits I have done over the last few years, this is the issue that has been raised most often by students. They rightly want regular feedback, a decent number of contact hours and access to the famous professors in their department. I want to see institutions seeking to attract students on the basis of teaching quality.

The Coalition's proposals are not a carbon copy of Lord Browne's, but they do encapsulate the key features of his model. From 2012-13, the first year of the new system, substantially more money will flow via students and less via HEFCE. At the same time, we will introduce a more progressive loans system and larger maintenance support, just as Browne recommended, to make sure no one is deterred from attending university on financial grounds. We will also improve the information available to prospective students and their families, so that they can make more informed decisions – as a first step, by introducing Key Information Sets, which will outline what is on offer in different courses at different universities in areas like student satisfaction, teaching time and graduate employment.

People are rightly asking for more information about how the new system will work in the longer term, rather than just in the first year. Our programme will reflect the Coalition's wider ambitions to reduce central political control, put more power in the hands of consumers and promote innovative delivery methods. The biggest lesson I have learnt in three decades as a policymaker is that letting new providers into the system is the single most powerful driver of reform. It is the rising tide that lifts all boats.

The very fact that universities don't get so much grant money and that money will follow learners opens up the system. But we also intend to move towards a single regulatory regime for providers of different types. This is likely to be of interest to the global higher education providers that already operate in many countries, as well as home-grown specialist institutions and perhaps even new liberal arts colleges.

In addition, we will end the fixed, yet illogical, link between degree-awarding powers and teaching. We have, perhaps unintentionally, created a regulatory system which says that awarding bodies must also teach students. That would be seen as absurd in any other part of the education sector. It is also ahistorical, for the past growth of higher education in England was based on colleges teaching students for external degrees. The polytechnics, for example, taught degrees examined by the old Council for National Academic Awards. This is a model with much going for it because it means students at new institutions can obtain degrees or other qualifications from prestigious and well understood institutions. Employers, in particular, are likely to value such clear signals. This is behind my support of initiatives like Pearson's exciting new BTEC degree, which will enable people to prove they have higher-level vocational skills.

We are also looking at options for freeing up student number controls. For example, one area of potential is tariff-based systems, in which entitlement to public support is linked to prior attainment. The initial response to the ambitious version proposed in the Browne report was not favourable. But are there some categories of students for whom a tariff approach could work, especially once the UCAS review is finished?

Our new student finance arrangements are clear. But reforming funding without liberalising the system so that students' choices become more meaningful would leave us, like Oscar Wilde's cynic, obsessed with price and ignorant of value. So we are equally committed to delivering a landscape in which public money isn't simply linked to students in an unresponsive way, but actually changes direction with the decisions they make.

David Willetts *is the UK Minister for Universities and Science.*

Who should pay for higher education – and how?

Bahram Bekhradnia

We have moved very rapidly in England from a situation where full-time undergraduate students paid nothing towards the cost of their higher education – that was the case until 1998 – to a position where students will in future pay 100% of their costs. That is the apparent effect of the new student finance regime that has been proposed by the government. Given that the philosophical basis for the introduction of fees in the first place was that the benefits of higher education should be shared between the state and the student, and therefore that it was right that the student should contribute to the cost, the implication of the state making no contribution would, on this logic, be that all the benefit is private, and that the state receives no benefit from educating graduates.

That would be the case if it were true that the state is not contributing anything to the cost of higher education. In fact, that is not the situation. What has changed is the basis on which the state will in future make its contribution, because the state will continue to contribute, just in a very different way. Additionally, it is possible – in fact the government claims that it is the case – that the balance between the amounts contributed by the state and the individual could change radically again at some point. At present higher education institutions (HEI's) receive grants directly from the government, through its intermediary the Higher Education Funding Council for England (HEFCE), and it also subsidises the loans that it provides students in order to pay their fees – subsequently being repaid through what is effectively a higher tax on the salaries of graduates.

In future the government has decided that it will not provide grants directly to universities but will provide funds to universities only by subsidising loans to students which they use to pay fees. This is a major ideological shift. It is presented by the government as increasing choice for students and providing funding to universities only insofar as students exercise choice and choose to go to that university, so also improving the incentive to provide high-quality education, be customer focused and so on. It is classic market economics. The reality though is that universities at present are funded only to the extent that they recruit students (that is the basis on which the government grant is given to universities). It could be that there will be some shift in the psychological state of students as they pay the money to universities themselves instead of the government, but even that is unknown. But it is highly debatable whether student choice will be affected at all. Nor is it at all likely that the government will achieve the sort of savings that it has claimed will accrue because of its withdrawal from providing grants directly to universities. As part of the package that included increased student fees and reduced government grant, the government has increased the maximum fee that universities may charge and with it the loans that it must provide to students. Additionally, at the same time it has reduced the amount that students must repay each month – despite the fact that they will have larger loans – while increasing the interest rate that they must pay, as well as the length of time over which they must pay as well. The balance is likely to be that an awful lot of people who take loans will not repay their loans in full. Consider too that the government's financial calculations were based on assumptions that average fees would be £7,500, whereas the reality appears to be that few universities will charge below that level. This means that the average will be much higher and therefore the cost to the government of the loans that it must make will be much higher too, all resulting in a recipe for much higher costs to the government than it had assumed.

There is no doubt that the government is in difficulty, and that the difficulty is born of ideology. The reality is that so long as loans are subsidised, the amount of loans that are taken, and the rules for paying back the loans, will make a difference to public expenditure. The government has to either moderate the level of the fees (and therefore the total amount of loans that it has to provide), or it has to regulate the number of students that are eligible for such loans. That is going to be a problem not just for this government in this country, but wherever this approach to funding is adopted.

The way that this government – and perhaps others following a similar path – thought that they would curb the level of fees was through straightforward market competition. Some universities would be unable to charge high fees because students would shun them and go to other universities which either had higher quality or better reputations, or lower prices. There are a number of problems with this approach. First, higher education is not a market like other markets. Higher education is a positional good, and it is not at all clear that there is the same sort of price elasticity in higher education as elsewhere. No doubt because of the changing job market where degrees are essential, students seem to be prepared to pay to go into higher education even though prices rise. A trebling of the fee in 2006 made no difference to demand. Allied to this is the fact that the government has set a price limit – the maximum fee is £9,000 - which narrows the band within which competition might take place. An oddity about higher education and the market is that there is some evidence that price is seen as a proxy for quality, which provides a disincentive for universities to reduce prices – as they might be seen as second rate. And finally, and perhaps most important, there is every indication that there is a large latent demand for higher education, and so even if some universities that have higher prestige take more students, those with less prestige are likely still to find that they have customers, even at prices that might seem at odds with their position in the market.

And that is why it is likely that the UK government will try to curb the number of people eligible for higher education – it will try to find a means of reducing the demand, and so force universities that do not have the reputation of some of their peers to compete for a limited market on the basis of price. These are extraordinary times, and the tectonic changes that are being introduced, almost haphazardly, are quite extraordinary. The stakes are high, and we are about to leap into the dark. What is certain however is that students of the future will pay a lot more for their education than in the past, and it could well be that opportunities to go to higher education are reduced as well. That does not sound like a good future outcome.

Bahram Bekhradnia is Director of HEPI, was formerly the Director of Policy at HEFCE for ten years and has advised twenty different national governments on the financing of higher education.

The Higher Education Policy Institute (HEPI) is the UK's only independent think tank devoted exclusively to higher education. Founded in 2002, HEPI has built up a strong reputation for robust and objective policy analysis and advice across a whole range of higher education issues. Its mission is to improve higher education in the UK by creating a better informed policy environment - informed by research and analysis, as well as drawing on experiences from other countries.

How a better HE funding system could make everybody happy

Johnny Rich

Minimal student debt, properly funded universities, low cost to the taxpayer and highly employable graduates available to recruiters at the right price. An impossible pipe dream, surely?

Actually, no. But unfortunately, such a confluence of virtues would indeed be impossible under the current HE funding system. That is because each is set at odds with another. For students to have low debts, the universities must go without funds or the taxpayer must foot the bill. And, as for employers, there's no driving force in the system to ensure students follow the paths they'd want, nor that universities should encourage them to do so.

And yet there is a way to align these interests. It all starts with looking at who benefits from higher education.

A little history

Once upon a time, people didn't need degrees. What training they needed was mostly delivered on the job. The cost of skilling the UK workforce was effectively met by its businesses. And they didn't mind because they were ensuring their employees could do their jobs.

But over the years, employees became more mobile and employers needed more flexibility. Employers also wanted staff with more formal qualifications and so got used to moving their investment from training to hiring. As the demand for graduates grew, the clamour among students for university places echoed more loudly too.

The UK expanded its HE system so that the country could serve this increasingly skilled, increasingly knowledge-based economy. And according to Lord Leitch's landmark review, by 2020 we will need to go even further to meet our future labour needs.[1] Half our jobs will be filled by individuals who have paid tens of thousands for the privilege of doing their jobs.

But many of those jobs will not be the ones they *expected* to get when they invested in their education. There are currently over 8,000 UK students studying forensic

---

1 Leitch Review: Prosperity for all in the Global Economy - World Class Skills, (TSO, 2006) suggested that by 2020 half of all jobs in the UK would be at graduate level.

science. There are only 9,500 jobs in the entire sector, and most of those are already filled – by chemistry and biology graduates.

Those eager CSI enthusiasts may well get jobs – well paid ones even – but, as with many other degrees, when they embarked on their financial adventure, it was on a false prospectus.

Because the expansion of HE since the 1980s represented a shift in the burden of cost from employer to student, it seemed only fair that the new courses should be the ones the students demanded. That way, no one could argue they weren't the prime beneficiaries of their education, surely? But no, because their information about, and understanding of, the labour market has been at best limited and at worst misguided.

Meanwhile, it's been costing taxpayers more too. After all, our economy and society needs graduates; doctors, social workers, and teachers. But, even though the taxpayer has been making a big contribution to the bill, we've had little say in whether HE would meet the nation's labour supply needs.

Make the funding follow the value

Higher education has three interdependent beneficiaries: the students who want rewarding careers, the nation which has social and economic needs, and the employers who need a highly skilled workforce. Why not let the economic benefits decide the balance of who pays? Indeed, why not let those same forces determine which universities are best at delivering benefits?

In other words, why not link the funding of universities directly to their ability to generate 'value'? It just so happens, the labour market has rather a good way of measuring value: it's called 'pay'.

So this is my big idea for the future: a graduate tax… but not as we know it. Instead of adding the cost of their education to the graduate's national insurance contribution (which, in effect, is the current repayment mechanism), add it to the employer's as a percentage of the graduate's pay. Then give that money back to the university where they studied and let them set their own student numbers.

Why it would work

If a graduate is highly employable, adding plenty of value to their employer, they will command a high salary and their university will be rewarded commensurately for their role in making them so valuable.

If however a university's graduates aren't proving to be a good source of revenue, the university will have to question what it's doing. Should it stop offering media studies, even though the student demand is there? Should it try to teach it better? Or, more likely, it would work harder to ensure the students recognise the employability skills they are picking up through their studies. Recruiters, who often complain that graduates may be well educated but aren't prepared for the workplace, may find universities are quick to change their priorities when their funding is at stake.

Lord Browne argued that employers' contribute through the premium they pay to graduates.[2] The question he didn't address is, what market forces might cause graduate salaries to rise if student debt increases? Workers are paid not according to their *need*, but according to their *value*.

Wider participation and student contributions

One of the key a dvantages is that this system would remove the principle barrier to entry into university: debt. Or more accurately, the fear of debt. It does not matter how 'progressive' the current funding system may be, able students from non-traditional backgrounds will never go to university in the desired numbers so long as the system *looks* too expensive, too risky and too complicated. Every *perceived* barrier needs to be removed, otherwise these students in particular will not even entertain the idea. They'll never discover that the financial hardship may be more manageable than they might believe.

Don't be mistaken however: the students would be contributing – probably just as much – but doing so *indirectly*. As the CBI would no doubt argue, higher taxes on employers will drive down graduate salaries to compensate. In other words, the total of pay and NI might be unaffected. This wouldn't bother the graduates: ask any student whether they'd rather earn £27k five years after graduation and owe £40k, or earn £25k and owe nothing. I'll give you odds they'll plump for the latter.

I said that students would *probably* contribute just as much. It is possible graduate pay would not fall. If Lord Leitch was right about the rising demand for graduates, the competition to recruit them may indeed keep their pay buoyant. If so, it would demonstrate that graduates really do offer sufficient value to their employers and, if that is indeed the case, it's only fair (for their sake and their universities') that they should be paid accordingly.

If on the other hand, graduates aren't worth it, they won't attract the salaries. The universities wouldn't get their funding and would stop producing so many graduates.

2   The Browne Report: Securing a Sustainable Future for Higher Education in England (DBIS, 2010)

Demand and supply would keep each other in check. Personally I believe more graduates *are* needed, not fewer, and their pay will hold steady, but if higher education isn't that valuable after all, we ought to let it contract.

But...

But what about the arts? What about social workers and nurses? Won't universities stop offering these courses because they don't command high salaries?

Firstly, the pay gap between arts and STEM courses is not as significant as some people imagine and the demand for courses and the salaries paid for those graduates will be led by the labour market. If the nation finds itself in need of nurses because universities don't want to teach them, it would have to start paying higher salaries to attract people into the profession, making it more worthwhile to teach those courses. In the short term, for certain 'reserved' professions, it would be consistent with the idea of 'the beneficiary pays' if the Government subsidised such courses directly to maintain labour supply. After all, taxpayers do benefit from good nursing.

Secondly, there are not endless numbers of students wanting to study STEM subjects. Universities have to respond to the supply of raw materials and they may find they can earn a better living teaching art history to students competing hard to join those courses than they can by churning out reluctant engineers. Arts courses cost much less to run and so, even with lower income, the financial margin may be greater.

There are of course other objections. Most can be answered. Some, probably, cannot. There is probably no perfect system of HE funding, but one thing is certain, the Government's current plan is a cart hurtling down a track. The stakeholders – students, universities, employers and taxpayers – are four horses pulling the cart, but each has been harnessed in a different way, pulling against the others. Sooner or later, this cart is going to end up in pieces or in a ditch. Unless our solution gives everyone a reason to pull in the same direction, then it's not a solution.

Johnny Rich is a media and higher education specialist with various roles as Publisher of brands such as Push (the leading independent resource for prospective students), Real World Magazine, the Recruiters' Guide to Courses & Campuses and the Oxbridge Students' Careers Resource. He is also a director of the Higher Education Academy. He appears regularly on television and radio as a specialist on students and higher education issues.

The future funding of higher education: has the Treasury got the sums wrong?

Pam Tatlow

Regardless of any Liberal-Democrat election manifesto promise, the die for higher fees was cast when George Osborne's October 2010 Comprehensive Spending Review (CSR) adopted the assumption that the public funding of teaching in English universities was a subsidy rather than an investment. In the ensuing and often heated debate about the impact on institutions, students and graduates, of allowing fees to rise to £9,000, surprisingly little has been said about the implications for the Exchequer, the taxpayer and the long-term sustainability of higher education funding in the future.

Accountancy vs economics

The primary reason why Osborne and Vince Cable, the BIS Secretary of State, settled on their approach was to reduce departmental spending - in other words, the planned Departmental Expenditure Limit (known as Resource DEL). The university teaching grant is counted directly within the Resource DEL, while *only* the estimated 'Accounting and Budgeting (RAB) charge' of student loans is counted within the DEL – in other words only the charge associated with the costs of providing these loans, taking into account repayments and write-off costs.[1]

Substituting tuition fee loans for the teaching grant will reduce BIS departmental expenditure by approximately 74% in the future. For example, if the RAB charge is approximately 26% and £2.8 billion of new fee loans are issued to replace a £2.8 billion reduction in teaching grant, the Department's Resource DEL falls by £2.072 billion per annum compared to the current DEL. In *accountancy* terms, the Osborne-Cable strategy achieves a reduction in departmental spending; however, given the changes to graduate repayments, this will be significantly less than the 74%. Furthermore, in *economic* terms this spending will simply be replaced in the future by borrowing, which has its own economic cost.[2]

---

1 The actual volume of new student loans issued is included within the Capital Annually Managed Expenditure (AME) item of the Departmental accounts (termed a financial asset)

2 The value of the new financial asset (i.e. new student loans) may be significantly lower than might currently be estimated when adopting the historic value of the RAB charge (approx 26.1%). The Department is committed to reviewing the estimate of the RAB charge if the estimate appears no longer to be accurate in estimating the level of interest rate subsidy or loan write off. Unless there is a fundamental improvement in either the earnings or employment outcomes of graduates in the future, it is probably the case that this financial asset will start to be significantly eroded at some point in the future. However, it may require several years to assess whether new borrowers do in fact require higher subsidies/write offs than the current cohorts of student loan recipients.

£13bn added to public sector net debt

There has been very little Parliamentary discussion about the requirement for this additional borrowing even though the independent Office of Budget Responsibility estimated in November 2010 that increasing tuition fees would require the Government to borrow £10.7 billion to fund student loans in 2015-16 compared to the £4.1 billion it borrowed in 2010-11. According to the OBR, these higher cash requirements will cumulatively add £13 billion to public sector net debt by 2015–16. The OBR's calculations took no account of the increased costs arising from last-minute concessions made by the Government prior to the House of Commons vote on fees in December 2010. These are likely to further increase the Treasury's borrowing requirement. Interestingly, the OBR did not adjust its November forecasts in March 2011 in spite of the fact that many universities have said that they intend to charge the maximum fee of £9,000 per annum in 2012 (rather than the £7,500 that BIS had banked on). This suggests that the OBR expects the Government to cut student numbers rather than stump-up the extra borrowing required to fund higher fees.

Student numbers, economic growth and tax receipts

A cut in the number of students would mean a decline in the number of those qualifying with graduate qualifications in the future, raising questions not only about the credibility of the Coalition's reform of higher education funding but also about the Government's understanding of the link between graduate qualifications, economic growth and tax receipts.

Risks to demand

So far, Osborne and Cable have said very little about the impact of the fee increases (albeit part mitigated by subsidised fee loans) on the wider economy. As an economist, Cable will appreciate that the most fundamental laws of economics suggest that, all other things being equal, tuition fee increases will result in a reduction in the quantity of higher education demanded. The extent to which demand will fall is a key issue. However, the elasticity of student demand – in other words the sensitivity of the market to price increases – was recently assessed[3]. The Institute For Fiscal Studies (IFS) concluded that an increase in tuition fees by £1,000 per annum – holding all other factors constant – would be expected to lead to a 4.4 *percentage point* decline in participation. The IFS also estimated that a £1,000 per annum increase in loans increases participation by 3.2 percentage points but that;

> "a £1,000 increase in loans or grants is not sufficient to counteract the impact of a £1,000 increase in fees – the coefficient on fees being significantly higher than both loans and grants.'

3   Dearden, L., Fitzsimons E., and Wyness, G. (2010), "The impact of the 2006-07 HE Finance reforms on HE participation", Department for Business innovation and Skills Research Paper Number 13, September 2010

In a nutshell, the higher fees in 2012 which are an inevitable consequence of Osborne's decision to withdraw taxpayer investment from university teaching, pose a real risk to demand.

Will the Exchequer be worse-off ?

The graduate earnings premium has been used by a succession of Ministers in the previous, as well as the current, Government to justify the introduction of graduate contribution systems. What is good for graduates is also good for the Treasury. It is not clear whether and how the Treasury and BIS have factored in the well-documented evidence of the net *Exchequer* benefit associated with undergraduate degree level provision[4]. Based on research commissioned by the Royal Society of Chemistry[5], this stands at approximately £81,875 (per graduate) overall in 2010 constant prices. If the IFS conclusions about the impact on demand of higher fees are correct, the total economic loss to the economy from the reduction in the number of graduates could be as much as £3.72 billion per annum in present value terms. Incorporating these wider economic impacts into the analysis implies that rather than the 2012-13 tuition fee and student support changes making the Exchequer *better off,* once the wider future taxation effects are considered, the Exchequer will be more than £2 billion per annum *worse off* in the future.

Public investment in education supported by OECD

The strong economic arguments in favour of the continued funding of undergraduate degrees by the Treasury, even at a time of austerity, was endorsed by the Organisation for Economic Co-operation and Development (OECD) in 2010 which concluded that;

> *"public investments in education, particularly at the tertiary level, are rational even in the face of running a deficit in public finances. Issuing government bonds to finance these investments will yield significant returns and improve public finances in the longer term.*[6]*"*

The decision to withdraw taxpayer investment from higher education teaching in English universities is therefore highly questionable.

---

4   The **gross Exchequer benefit** represents the present value of the benefits to the Exchequer associated with the provision of an undergraduate degree relative to an individual in possession of 2 or more GCE 'A-Levels'. The present value of the Exchequer benefits associated with a degree is characterised by the enhanced tax, National Insurance and VAT paid by an individual over their lifetime relative to possession of 2 or more GCE 'A-Levels' in present value terms. The **net Exchequer benefit** is the gross Exchequer benefit minus the present value of the Exchequer costs associated with funding a degree. These costs include the direct costs (such as HEFCE funding and student support) and indirect costs (foregone taxation receipts during qualification attainment).

5   Royal Society of Chemistry and Institute of Physics (2005), 'The economic benefits of higher education qualifications', a report produced by PricewaterhouseCoopers LLP, January 2005

6   OECD *Education at a Glance 2010*

Whatever the wider benefits of higher education to society (and there are many) there is no sound *economic* case for the wholesale withdrawal of direct taxpayer investment from higher education teaching. On the contrary, the short-term 'gains' pursued by Osborne and Cable to reduce the Departmental Expenditure Limit appear to be little more than a mirage which obscures much higher net borrowing and future losses to the taxpayer. Being clever with the accounts is no substitute for taking an economic view of what counts and the current plans are unlikely to provide a sound basis on which to either build the economy or secure the future long-term sustainability of higher education in England.

Pam Tatlow *is Chief Executive of the university think-tank,* million+ *and has worked at a senior level in education, health and public affairs*

million+ *engages in advocacy and publishes research and analysis with the aim of ensuring that individuals from every walk of life have opportunities to benefit from access to universities which excel in teaching, research and knowledge exchange*

The challenges facing the UK's world-class universities and the importance of diversity

Wendy Piatt

The UK's leading research-intensive universities are playing a critical role as the UK works and thinks its way back to sustainable economic growth. Our economic competitiveness is underpinned by a higher education system which is recognised internationally for the excellence of its research and educational provision. The UK's research performance, and the attractiveness of the UK to overseas researchers, students, and inward investment, is in no small part because the UK is home to a significant number of the world's leading research-intensive universities.

There is a well-developed body of evidence which has examined the importance and characteristics of world-class universities.[1] World-class universities are characterised by a high concentration of excellence, talent and infrastructure; they generate multidisciplinary research, provide a focal point for clusters of economic activity, and deliver highly skilled people to the labour market. In doing so, they make a significant contribution to a nation's knowledge base, economy and international competitiveness. The UK's leading research-intensive universities utilise their critical mass of talent and infrastructure to generate real benefits to the UK economy, and are essential to the health of the higher education sector. However, the UK cannot afford to be complacent. Our higher education sector faces an unprecedented set of challenges, all of which threaten to erode the UK's long-standing success in higher education and research.

The first challenge is increased costs. There is evidence of severe cost pressures across the teaching and research activities of Russell Group institutions.[2] Ongoing investment is required to maintain a world-class learning experience, with research-intensive universities facing cost pressures on teaching, particularly in relation to challenges posed by an increasingly digital world. The nature of research is also changing. Research challenges have become increasingly complex, cutting across a number of different disciplines, and are global in their scope. Therefore there has been a rise in the need for collaborating internationally and across disciplines. Also, advances in technology have fuelled a need for better and more sophisticated equipment. All of these factors have increased the cost of research.

The second major challenge is increased global competition. Developed and developing nations are increasingly prioritising research and higher education as they seek to

---

1   Salmi, J. *The challenge of establishing world-class universities* World Bank (2009) examines this literature in more detail

2   Russell Group *Staying on top: the challenge of sustaining world-class higher education in the UK* (2010)

create more skilled workforces, stimulate socio-economic mobility and strengthen their economic competitiveness.[3] There are already signs that the UK could be falling behind; we now produce fewer papers than both the US and China and there has been rapid growth in research from non-G8 nations. The UK's share of world publications has fallen since 1999, and in 2008 was less than 8%.[4]

Several of our competitors have prioritised government expenditure to support higher education and research. The US and France have chosen to use stimulus packages to invest in their leading universities to underpin long-term economic growth, and a recent speech by President Obama reaffirmed his intention for the USA;

"to out-innovate, out-educate, and out-build the rest of the world.[5]"

Not only are countries seeking to invest more, they are seeking to invest more selectively. Much attention has been given to efforts in Asia, with initiatives in China and South Korea aiming to transform existing institutions into world-class universities. But these efforts are also occurring elsewhere in Europe. Germany is focussing on funding clusters of excellence to promote top-level research, and France is developing centres of excellence to compete at the international level. Denmark has completely restructured its public research base to create a smaller number of institutions that have critical mass comparable to other leading universities in Europe.

With other countries investing billions of pounds in their leading universities, even before any cuts in the 2010 Comprehensive Spending Review (CSR) were announced, the UK was in real danger of losing its international competitive edge. When these significant reductions to funding were announced, the importance of averting a potential crisis in UK higher education became even more urgent. Given these cuts, the Government's plans for introducing higher contributions in England are therefore the only viable way forward, so that the UK's leading universities have a fighting chance of remaining world-class, and being able to compete with the world's best universities. However, it is important to recognise that there will be a funding shortfall after the cuts really kick in and before universities are able to access any new fee income.

Income generated by the new fees regime will help the UK maintain a world-class student experience, by supporting the higher costs of excellent research-led teaching. The UK's leading universities need funding to innovate and set the pace of change in university teaching if they are to remain amongst the world's best. A system of graduate contributions

---

3   Douglass, J. *Higher education's new global order* Centre for Studies in Higher Education (2009)

4   Department for Business, Innovation and Skills *International comparative performance of the UK research base* (2009)

5   Obama, B. *State of the Union address* (2011)

should also facilitate a more diverse market in higher education, where differing models of teaching and learning can be efficiently supported. Graduate contributions provide more incentives for institutions to improve quality and their responsiveness to students' needs, as contributions encourage students to be more demanding of their universities. The retention of a cap on fees will, however, limit the extent of the diversity and dynamism generated by the new regime.

At a time of fiscal austerity, it makes sense to target public funds by building on success rather than trying to spread limited funds too thinly. Funding for research, knowledge transfer and capital needs to be concentrated on institutions with the necessary critical mass, quality of research and excellence in provision, and who are best placed to compete with the rest of the world. This will ensure that the support for the UK's world-class universities is sustained, and that the whole of the UK's diverse higher education system continues to enjoy the international recognition it rightly deserves.

A higher education system which embraces diversity rather than homogeneity will enable the UK to compete effectively in a global economy. The needs and demands of employers differ widely, therefore the higher education sector, and the courses it offers, should reflect this diversity. Professor Alison Wolf has argued:

> *"To support research and innovation, countries need a sizable, but not vast, number of top-class, superbly trained researchers and developers, not a very large number of imperfectly trained ones.[6]"*

It is only by continuing to meet the broad range of needs of the economy that the UK can hope to maintain its global competitiveness in the face of ever increasing competition. President Obama has set the challenge that the US intends to out-innovate, out-educate and out-build the rest of the world. The UK must rise to this challenge, and not lose its hard-won comparative advantage.

Dr Wendy Piatt is Director General of The Russell Group. She was previously Deputy Director and head of public service reform at the Prime Minister's Strategy Unit where she has also led work on social mobility, education and skills, local government and digital inclusion. Prior to that, she was Head of Education Policy at the Institute for Public Policy Research, specialising in higher and further education.

The Russell Group represents 20 leading UK universities which are committed to maintaining the very best research, an outstanding teaching and learning experience and unrivalled links with business and the public sector.

---

6   Wolf, A. *Does education matter?* (2002)

UK higher education as a strategic national asset

Paul Clark

The UK is currently experiencing the most severe retrenchment in public spending since the Second World War. While the higher education sector is not immune to the effects of this fiscal pressure, it has escaped relatively lightly compared to other areas of public service in terms of headline public investment figures. Government investment in science and research will remain constant in cash terms up to 2015, at £4.6 billion a year (still a 9 per cent cut in real terms). And while direct grant funding for higher education in England is to be cut by 25 per cent by 2015, reforms were voted through to replace this funding stream with a system of income-contingent loans for students funded by the government, allowing universities to charge student fees of up to £9000 for UK students from 2012 – much higher than at present.

Thus by 2015 the university sector could see overall levels of funding at least maintained, while other critical public services face significant reductions. There is a very good reason for maintaining this level of investment: a strong and vibrant higher education sector is essential for driving the economic growth that the UK will need to recover from recession and compete in the global marketplace.

Recognising this as the sector's primary purpose is just one of the major shifts in higher education policy to have taken place recently, one which will set a new course over the next decade and possibly beyond. In this changed environment, higher education is conceived of and treated in policy terms as a strategic national asset, an industry every bit as essential for the economy as financial services, manufacturing, or retail have been in the recent and more distant past.

This new role was recently enshrined in the government's Plan for Growth, published alongside the 2011 budget:

> *Higher education is central to economic growth and the UK has one of the most successful higher education systems in the world.*[1]

The opportunities for the sector were also set out in a report from the McKinsey Global Institute, which looked at long-term economic priorities for the UK:

---

1   Plan for Growth, HMT, March 2011 (http://cdn.hm-treasury.gov.uk/2011budget_growth.pdf)

Traditional debates about education have focused on its crucial role as a public service, increasing skills and ensuring fair opportunity for all... But if we view education through a different lens – that of an industry – then the UK education sector has many of the characteristics of a very promising growth opportunity.[2]

Research from Universities UK demonstrates the scale of the economic contribution of the HE sector– contributing around £59 billion to the UK economy overall[3]. In terms of export activities alone, UK universities generate around £2.2 billion in non-EU student tuition fees, which places this source of income in the UK's top 20 most valuable export products[4]. International students also generate an additional £2.3 billion in off-campus expenditure.

In future, this contribution is only likely to increase, as demand for higher skills increases, more diverse connections are made between universities and businesses – both nationally and in their locality, and the UK benefits from the expansion of the global market in higher education. The international student market is set to grow by around 7 per cent a year on average. In 2009 alone, the number of international students increased by 12 per cent, from 2.96 million to 3.43 million[5]. While the US share of this market has declined in recent years, that of the UK (its closest rival) has held steady, meaning that the UK is well-placed in terms of potential future growth. International students are foot-soldiers in the global war of ideas, and the UK needs to ensure that it can compete effectively. Moreover, UK higher education has a strong international brand, and the benefits generated through this industry flow to all regions. In short, it has all the hallmarks of a highly attractive investment opportunity.

Successive UK governments will need to ensure they have in place a strategic and policy framework which on the one hand facilitates domestic and international investment in higher education, while on the other provides the right regulatory structure for the sector to flourish. This means placing a continuing emphasis on self-direction for the UK's universities, providing the right incentives for sustainable growth, and continuing to encourage greater transparency in operations and service delivery.

One of the main reasons for maintaining this tight political and economic focus is that the sector faces fierce competition over the long term. This applies as much in

---

2   From Austerity to Prosperity: Seven priorities for the long term, McKinsey Global Institute, November 2010 (http://www.mckinsey.com/mgi/publications/uk_report/index.asp)

3   The Impact of Universities on the UK Economy, UUK, November 2009 (http://www.universitiesuk.ac.uk/Publications/Pages/ImpactOfUniversities4.aspx)

4   UK Exports: General Trade: Top 20 products by SITC, HMRC, November 2010

5   Unesco Institute for Statistics, 2009

the domestic arena as it does internationally. Many countries have woken up to the economic potential of investment in tertiary education, and its importance in driving innovation and skills growth, and there is no room for the UK to be complacent.

In a time of scarce resources, universities are competing for domestic attention with other 'core' spheres of public service – schools, hospitals, transport, the police and emergency services, to name a handful. Many of these services play a very prominent role and impact daily on people's lives. The contribution that universities make to public life is substantial, in terms of health, well-being, and citizenship, but this is often less immediately visible than the local A&E service or police officer on the street. The higher education sector needs to work that much harder to ensure that it secures an appropriate share of government resources, and that its economic and wider social contribution is fully recognised.

Internationally, the competition is even stronger, as the UK's major economic competitors are investing heavily in their own tertiary education systems. In the recent past, the UK has looked across the Atlantic to keep an eye on its primary competitor, but this position is changing as the global balance of power shifts to the Far East. By 2027, the Chinese economy will be as large as that of the US; by 2032 the BRIC[6] countries combined will be as large as the G7[7]; and not long thereafter the so-called N-11[8] countries will also rival the G7[9]. China and India are also catching up very fast with the EU in terms of research and innovation performance, further strengthening their position in the new order of the global knowledge economy.

This shift eastwards in economic influence is also reflected in changes to the international hierarchy of urban power. Cities are essential to economic growth, and attract to themselves substantial investment – this is never truer than when they are centred around a strong university system. One only has to think of the economic power of Los Angeles in the US, or Oxford in the UK. But by 2025, more than 20 of the world's top 50 cities ranked by GDP will be in Asia, up from 8 in 2007.[10] In this new ranking, three of the world's top 10 cities will be in China, with Shanghai leapfrogging London as an economic powerhouse.

There is now very strong evidence of the direct connection between cities and

---

6   The so-called BRIC countries are: Brazil, Russia, India, and China.

7   The members of the G7 are: Canada, France, Germany, Italy, Japan, the UK, and the US.

8   The members of the N-11 group (standing for 'Next 11', behind the BRIC countries in terms of economic growth) are: Bangladesh, Egypt, Indonesia, Iran, Mexico, Nigeria, Pakistan, Philippines, South Korea, Turkey, and Vietnam

9   The Long-term Outlook for the BRICs and N-11 Post-Crisis, Goldman Sachs Global Economics Paper 192, December 2009 (http://www2.goldmansachs.com/ideas/brics/long-term-outlook-doc.pdf)

10 Urban World: Mapping the economic power of cities, McKinsey Global Institute, March 2011

universities in terms of driving economic growth. One only has to look at the recent decision by the Bloomberg administration in New York City to invest in the development and operation of a new applied science and engineering research campus in that city – a competition which thus far has attracted interest from prestigious universities around the world, including Stanford University in the US, the Indian Institute of Technology in Mumbai, and the University of Warwick in the UK. Commenting on the development and its importance to the economy of New York City, Harvard economics professor Edward L. Gleiser wrote:

"The late Senator Daniel Patrick Moynihan of New York is often credited with saying that the way to create a great city is to "create a great university and wait 200 years," and the body of evidence on the role that universities play in generating urban growth continues to grow.[11]"

Against this shifting domestic and global background, the opportunities for the higher education sector to strengthen and enhance the UK's overall global economic position are immense. The same is true for a number of advanced and emerging economies. But the potential threats for the UK are also significant.

One of the most significant risks concerns the UK government's policy on student immigration. The government made a public commitment to reduce net migration to the UK. Once in power, major reviews of the primary channels into the UK for migrants took place, including a review of the student route. The policy proposals which emerged as a result sought broadly to protect universities from the clamp-down on numbers, recognising the economic, academic, and cultural benefits of preserving strong global academic ties. Nevertheless, experience from the US shows that the damage could already have been done, as the message is communicated around the world that the UK is not welcoming to international students. The US has still to regain the market share of international students it enjoyed prior to the visa restrictions imposed after 9/11, with the current figure stubbornly 5 percentage points below the level in 2000. The UK must avoid the same fate.

The policy response therefore needs to ensure a number of things to maintain the global status of this strategic national industry. These prescriptions build on the existing strengths of the UK system, but could easily be applied to other sectors around the world.

First, the quality of the overall brand needs to be maintained, through appropriate regulation and a focus on institutional self-direction – one of the key strengths of the

11 New York Times Economix blog post (http://economix.blogs.nytimes.com/2011/03/22/done-right-a-new-applied-science-center-for-new-york-makes-sense/?hp)

UK sector. Second, overall resource levels need to be sustained at least, now and into the future, so that higher education commands its share of public investment. Third, the regulatory structure needs to play to the sector's strengths and not act as a barrier – this applies to issues ranging from student visa control, to intellectual property, to data collection and transparency. Fourth, a joined-up response is required across government departments which have an interest in preserving the health and strength of the university system – currently the Department for Business, Innovation, and Skills, but also including Treasury, the Foreign and Commonwealth Office, the Cabinet Office, and the Home Office. A long-term, coordinated effort is required across a range of political fronts and across Party lines.

With the right policy framework in place, one which genuinely treats UK higher education as a prized national asset, universities can continue to cement their place at the heart of the economy, and occupy this newly-inhabited role with more and more confidence. In return, the sector will continue to deliver financial and economic benefits to the regions in which they're located; to the UK nationally through skills growth, R&D, and effective business interaction; and internationally, by securing the UK's position as one of the leaders of the global knowledge economy throughout the next century.

Paul Clark is Director of Policy at Universities UK where he is responsible for coordinating the organisation's full range of policy and research activity, working to influence national developments in higher education, and shaping the future policy agenda.

Universities UK is the representative organisation for the UK's universities. Founded in 1918, its mission is to be the definitive voice for all universities in the UK, providing high quality leadership and support to its members to promote a successful and diverse higher education sector.

Section two – How can we broaden the debate?

Striving for excellence in a new world

Alan Langlands

I welcome this invitation to do some 'blue skies' thinking about higher education, for two reasons. First, if we are to believe some commentators, the dominant weather pattern for higher education in England is decidedly overcast and unsettled, with thunderclouds looming as we head towards the new funding system in 2012-13. Without underestimating the considerable challenges that lie ahead, my own forecast is for a sunnier outlook; universities change lives and they will remain a pre-requisite for a vibrant economy and a just society.

Second, the preoccupation with the new funding settlement and its associated reforms has diverted attention from the bigger picture – the global context in which we are operating, the principles that underpin our work, and the need to keep building for the future. Universities and colleges must continue to focus on these longer-term issues, responding actively to social, economic, technological and cultural developments and opportunities.

Let me deal first with funding. HEFCE has allocated a total of £6.5 billion for teaching, research and capital projects in 2011-12 – an overall reduction, in cash terms, of 9.5 per cent. This is a challenging settlement, but universities and colleges have been preparing for it for some time, and we know that the sector is in good financial shape with strong cash balances and reserves. Total income in universities grew by 5.7 per cent in 2009-10 confirming, yet again, their success in attracting international research funding and overseas students, and the importance of the postgraduate economy.

The implications of the shift to the new system, where the bulk of funding for teaching in higher education will be routed through the student loan system, are as yet largely unknown, although my view is that if demand and participation levels hold up, university and college incomes will continue to grow. HEFCE is working with Government, the sector and our partner agencies to ensure a smooth transition to the new arrangements.

That said, public investment in higher education in this country remains stubbornly below the Organisation of Economic Co-operation and Development (OECD) average, at a time when the developing economies to the East, the commodity producers, and most other established economies in the West, are all investing. My strongly-held view is that the UK Government must return to the question of public investment in higher education as the economy improves. Of course, universities and colleges must demonstrate the very significant contribution they are making (circa £60 billion per annum) to economic recovery and growth, as well as confirming that higher learning can be enriching, enlarging and inspiring – the enduring watermark of a civilised society.

This brings me to the 'bigger picture'. Universities and colleges are international gathering points for a range of important discussions: about climate change, technological and medical advances, the impact of demographic, political and social change, the pursuit of artistic excellence. In research, the UK punches well above its weight: with 1 per cent of global population the UK receives 12 per cent of the world's science and research citations. We also have an excellent track record of business-related research, working with industrial, commercial and third sector partners to stimulate economic growth and build social capital.

Our primary objective must be to build on this success. HEFCE is playing its part in this. As the biggest single funder of research in the UK (investing £1.6 billion every year), we have increased our support for internationally excellent and world-leading research. We are maintaining our emphasis on knowledge exchange, innovation and enterprise activity and we will, through targeted teaching funding, continue to promote widening participation and protect high cost subjects, specialist institutions and disciplines that might struggle in a pure market economy.

To my mind a number of key principles underpin the current and future success of higher education. They are:

- *Opportunity*: people with the potential to benefit from successful participation in higher education should have the opportunity to do so, regardless of background or social class. The proportion of young people recruited from the most disadvantaged parts of the country has increased by about 30 per cent over the past five years. It is important to maintain this momentum. We will need to keep a close eye on the impact of the new fee regime, and on ensuring that the new initiatives on access and student support deliver their intended objectives. Universities should be an engine for social mobility rather than a means of entrenching privilege.

- *Choice*: universities and colleges must ensure that students have the information they need to make informed choices and provide a diverse and flexible range of provision embracing all academic disciplines. This diversity will include more private sector organisations. This is subject to policy discussion at the moment, but in my view the deal should be clear – the status of an institution with designated higher education programmes should not affect the ability of students to access student funding or the ability of the institution to apply for public funding for teaching, subject to the requirements of whatever regulatory framework is put in place in relation to access, quality, information and financial sustainability. Greater plurality that injects innovation, expertise and high quality education will be welcome.

○ *Quality*: teaching 'quality' is defined in terms of learning opportunities: ensuring that appropriate and effective teaching, support and assessment is in place for students. HEFCE has a statutory responsibility to ensure that the quality of teaching and learning is assessed fairly but universities are responsible for standards. They must continue to work hard with their students to improve every aspect of their educational experience. High quality research with economic and social impact will be at the heart of the new Research Excellence Framework (REF) and performance will drive our innovation funding.

Finally, institutional autonomy will remain the bedrock of success in higher education. We need a balanced approach to regulation that protects the interests of students and the wider public but real progress depends on enhancing the freedom of institutions to inspire their students and to work for continuous improvement in learning and teaching, research and knowledge exchange.

Sir Alan Langlands is the Chief Executive of HEFCE. He was formerly the Principal and Vice-Chancellor of the University of Dundee (2000-2009) and Chief Executive of the National Health Service (NHS) in England (1994-2000).

The Higher Education Funding Council for England (HEFCE) promotes and funds high-quality teaching and research in universities and colleges with higher education programmes.

A Five-Point Plan for the future of higher education

James Ladyman

The culture of higher education has changed dramatically in the last few decades. Changes introduced to increase accountability and improve the quality of both teaching and research have had unintended consequences. The drive for procedures and processes, where once there were simply judgments and decisions, may have raised some standards and eliminated some shoddy or even corrupt practice. However, the elevation of the mechanisms to ensure the correct use of academic expertise, to the status of substituting for it, undermines intellectual values and ultimately quality. It is also a pointless waste of money. Like the impact agenda, it is worse than wrong, it is stupid. Our universities are precious institutions making up one of the only sectors of the UK that can truly claim to be world class. We need politicians who don't want to be radical with higher education but conservative. Otherwise we will quickly lose one of our greatest positional advantages in the global economy, one made all the more valuable by the status of the English language. The threat is manifested by the shallow *managerialese* with which our once ivory towers resound. Here are my five ideas for the future of higher education.

1) Strip away bureaucracy and management

The UK research councils are heavily invested in the management and administration of academic research, just as the Quality Assurance Agency (QAA) and associated organisations are invested in the management and administration of teaching. Many of these institutions are engaged in classic rent-seeking activity. This is why the applications forms for postgraduate scholarships are redesigned each year, to the great consternation (and investment of time) by those of us who have to complete them. This is why there is always a need for another document with a vision of the future, no matter how ephemeral and epiphenomenal the last one turned out to be. We need to stop the endless profusion of strategy documents and cull the cohorts of research managers and skills trainers.

The trend has been for the research councils to move simultaneously towards larger and larger grants, and to move from responsive mode, where applications in any area are considered on their merits, to strategic mode, where some currently fashionable area is designated and applications are solicited. Both of these movements lead to less efficiency and stifled innovation. Large grants concentrate resources and lead to teams of people supposedly generating large amounts of research. However, in many cases the people who ostensibly lead them stop thinking about the research topic the moment the grant application is in and move on to the next one. In reality, teams of postdoctoral researchers and more junior staff are left to do the actual work. The grant will involve lots of resources for administration, workshops and conferences and, because the research council has invested so heavily, there is an alignment of interests as both they and the recipient talk up the results of the project that may have delivered substantially less than promised.

On the other hand, small grants are extremely efficient since they involve paying a modest amount to free an individual researcher from teaching and administration for a relatively short amount of time. That person then has a massive personal incentive to work to full effect since he or she knows this is his or her chance to get some research done, and there is little potential for waste. However, this might provide fewer flagship projects to put in the research council glossy brochure, reduce the need for research infrastructure and diminish the role for the research council all round. No need for leadership training courses for the senior investigators, and a much less onerous and therefore cheaper application process. No need too for the infrastructure that all universities have created to service applications for large grants and to interact with the bloated bureaucracies of the research councils.

2) Terminate the impact agenda

The idea of assessing research according to its likely social and economic impact is just the idea of picking winners, and that is what science itself does, in part by institutional processes such as peer review, open exchange and discussion of ideas, independent third party scrutiny of evidence and so on. The idea that one of the greatest achievements of collective human endeavour, that took millennia to evolve through the advancement of our greatest minds, is somehow going to be enhanced by the research councils adopting the slogan 'excellence with impact', and churning out blather about end-users and engagement, would be laughable were it not so counter to the national interest. The best way to maximize the economic impact of science is to have a thriving culture of pure research that is left alone.

Nobody is saying that the government cannot decide to invest huge amounts in the equivalent of more efficient candle making, but some scientists and other intellectuals need to be allowed to pursue ideas for their own sake. That is what has saved us in the past, as Margaret Thatcher noted when she defended academic independence by pointing out that the useless boffins in our universities were precisely the people who gave us radar and code-breaking when we needed both most. The research councils now insist that all applicants think about end-users at an early stage of their research, which is pointless for those of us who work on esoteric and abstract issues that are only of interest to other specialists. Such research will produce enough of a return to easily justify the relatively small outlay, but we cannot predict exactly what that will be other than by considering academic quality. Raising quality is vital to achieve most goals associated with academic inquiry and it is necessary but not sufficient for good teaching. However the impact agenda, like the large grant culture, encourages superficiality, spin and hype at the expense of core intellectual values. The best predictor of economic and societal impact is academic excellence.

When it comes to public engagement and meeting the educational needs of the population, putting pressure on already stretched academics is not the answer. The last government took away resources and effectively killed off continuing education programmes that enhanced communities and universities. Modest funds would restore them in the future.

The introduction of the Research Assessment Exercise (RAE) is recognised to have had unintended consequences because it massively changed the incentive structure for academics and universities. Teaching became less of a priority as investing more in it brought no direct rewards, whereas failing to have sufficient 'high quality' publications for the RAE had a massive cost. The impact agenda is again changing the incentive structure substantially, this time not by prioritising one internal good over another, but by making the external good of 'impact' of paramount importance. This is likely to have substantial negative effects on academic quality and therefore will not increase impact. Again resources are being wasted by universities investing in infrastructure to service the impact agenda.

3) Restore the prestige and value of scholarship

There is an old-fashioned kind of scholar that is completely undervalued in the contemporary university. They may lack ambition and networking skills, nor know the latest 'impact factor' ranking of different journals. They may have published relatively little and they may have scant appetite for climbing the managerial ladder. What they do is study their subjects for their whole lives. They treat embarking upon teaching a second year course on a subject as a reason to read and learn themselves, not merely as a distraction to be dismissed on the way to filling in another grant application. The categories of high flyer and scholar are not exclusive, but there are many high flyers whose work is relatively ephemeral and whose learning will never really deepen beyond a certain point, and there are many scholars who are not high flyers for most of their careers but who produce work of lasting value, sometimes becoming celebrated in their mature years or even after their demise. The pressure to burn bright as an academic star in early and mid career threatens to kill off such people. We are creating selection pressures for academics to be socially adept, charismatic networkers, but will likely select for fewer and/or less clever people.

4) End the permanent revolution in administrative structures

Some universities have undergone multiple reorganisations in recent years as fads for schools, colleges, departments or faculties wax and wane. Sprinkle in lots of waffle about interdisciplinary synergies and elaborate boxologies that model the interactions among staff, students and administrators and you have a recipe for a lot of waste. Then consider the specialists in transformation management and the change consultants that you will need to hire to help your staff through the trauma of adapting to new ways of working, designed by people who know nothing about how things really work. However, don't worry, the staff development people will put on a reflexology course to help get you through it all. Academics know what works, please leave them to it.

5) Stop the drive to formalise processes and make judgment criteria explicit

Now one doesn't just mark an essay, write comments and talk to the student about it. One must also give it separate marks for some more or less arbitrary list of criteria such as independence, knowledge, clarity, argument or perhaps even, scholarly values. We are supposed to be making explicit our actual judgment, which is fine in so far as an overall judgment will be based on those sorts of criteria, except that it does not follow that we really arrive at an overall mark by aggregating separate marks for them. In reality what we do of course it mark the essay and then think up the marks for the criteria, but this takes time and is one tiny example of the myriad ways in which processes and forms waste time and falsify the nature of what we do. Many such changes have been introduced without any evidence that they will improve anything and without regard to their cost.

The latest fad is the idea of a 'workload' model. For those of us who think models are things like the billiard ball model of a gas, or the liquid drop model of the nucleus, these sorts of things come as a bit of a shock. They don't come with predictive power, precision or accuracy. They don't even describe the phenomena adequately. However, they are treated as if they were empirical data about how much work we are doing. The fact that they are wildly inaccurate is not allowed to get in the way of the drive towards centralised command and control, so better to tell the staff to adjust their perceptions. To think otherwise would be to suggest that the university would make decisions on the basis of pseudoscience.

So there are my five ideas for the future of higher education, I think those who know the sector best, academics, might agree.

Professor James Ladyman is Professor of Philosophy at the University of Bristol and is Co-Editor of The British Journal for the Philosophy of Science.

What should higher education be for?

Charles Seaford, Laura Stoll and Louis Coiffait

In the foreword of his recent report on UK higher education funding, Lord Browne wrote that:

> *"the return to graduates for studying will be on average around 400%".*

In this world view higher education is an economic investment, and there is and should be pressure to take a high paying job. Indeed it would be *inefficient* for graduates to take lower paid jobs: the market, as manifest in salary scales, is the best way of allocating scarce resources. The resulting headlines focus on debates about tuition fees, scholarships and Return on Investment (ROI).

The dominance of this narrow market-based lens for viewing higher education is in danger of crowding out alternative or more rounded views – potentially damaging the well-being of individual graduates and whole nations permanently. Is there really nothing more to life than the bottom line? As the philosopher AC Grayling warns, are universities really the;

> *"mere continuation of school for the same sausage-machine purpose of churning out employees"*

Don't we need qualified people who are prepared to take relatively low paid jobs, especially in the public and voluntary sectors? Don't the benefits of higher education extend to wider society, beyond individual graduates? Don't we value the personal and intellectual development that higher education provides for its own sake – and want to make it available to as many people as possible rather than just those who have, or are aiming to make, lots of money?

There are really two questions here which are connected but distinct. The first is what should higher education be for? And the second is how should we pay for it? There is a lot of public debate about the second, but perhaps not enough of the first. Many of us have an uneasy feeling that underlying Browne's stance is the view that higher education, when not delivering clearly job-related skills, is a *luxury*, pursued for pleasure or entertainment (a point highlighted by Margaret Thatcher's famous statement to that effect on meeting a Norse Literature student). Some subsidies for skill development are justified (where there is an identifiable market failure or where a subject is 'strategically important and vulnerable') but why should we care too much about the luxury side: surely this can be left to the market and consumer choice?

But non-job-related education is not entertainment. Its goal from individuals' point of view is not to provide pleasure but to prepare them to lead 'the good life', enabling those around them to do the same. In reality the distinction between learning job-related skills and other parts of higher education is overstated: the skills needed for 'work' and the skills needed for 'life' are often the same, and in any case, the evidence shows that jobs are often an important part of the good life – both in terms of income and in giving people a sense of purpose or meaning. Beyond this, people may disagree what exactly the good life is but they tend to agree that it is a good thing and that everyone is entitled to it. Educators need to be clear that, like health care professionals, they make a vital contribution to it. It is true that as things stand, not everyone will benefit significantly from higher education in this way – and perhaps not every higher education institution (HEI) is capable of delivering this kind of benefit. But let no-one who *has* benefited deny the possibility that others less fortunate will one day be able to do so. This is what higher education is for – and for as many people as possible.

Alongside these contributions to individuals' lives there are benefits of higher education which are best considered at the societal level. These obviously include the gains to the economy as a whole via its role in attracting the capital and skilled workers necessary for the UK to remain competitive in the global market. But higher education also leads to better quality goods and services (including public service provision). Links (and student transfers) between institutions allow important international relationships to be fostered. It also brings wider cultural benefits to society, including the diffusion of knowledge through schooling, public education and the arts; and it enables increased levels of social mobility.

However Lord Browne and his fellow-travellers have a trump card. Advocates of this broader view of education have not agreed on what they mean by the good life, let alone how to measure whether higher education is indeed preparing people to live it or to deliver these wider social goods. By contrast it is relatively easy to measure the earnings potential created by this or that degree course (not completely straightforward but *relatively* easy) and to devise a way of holding HEI's to account for delivering it (market based, i.e. using student fees). As management guru Peter Drucker famously wrote, what gets measured gets done.

So let us try to meet these criticisms. We believe the good life is one in which people *flourish*. This means they relate well with the people and the world around them, and as a result have good feelings and a sense of satisfaction with their life as a whole. This idea dates back to Aristotle, who couched it in terms of excellence, meaning fulfilling one's nature. More recently psychologists Ryan and Deci[1] have couched it in terms

1   Ryan R and Deci E (2000) Self-determination theory and the facilitation of intrinsic motivation, social development and well-being. American Psychologist 55, 68-78

of 'functioning' and satisfaction of 'psychological needs'. These needs are satisfied by relationships, autonomy – or freedom from restriction, and a sense of purpose, meaning and competence. Money can play a part in all of those things but it's not an end of itself.

Whether these needs are satisfied depends partly on a person's circumstances – employment status, level and stability of income, housing conditions, education and so on. Also important are an individual's personal resources – things like optimism, emotional resilience, self-esteem and health. These are largely innate but can also be affected by how people behave and feel and what they experience – there is a feedback loop. In short, the good life is one where individuals' social and economic circumstances together with their personal resources lead to experiencing high levels of well-being.

Higher education contributes to this in a variety of ways: it contributes to the material prosperity of alumni and of society more widely; it (to varying degrees) removes class and location based barriers to opportunity; but it also contributes to an individual's personal resources in ways that allow them to feel capable, to pursue meaningful activities, to have aesthetic experiences[2], to feel a degree of autonomy.

There is nothing very remarkable in this list. The various contributions itemised are the objectives of many if not most educators. There is also well established practical understanding, if not always agreement, of how to achieve them. What is important is that they are based on a more solid foundation than any purely economic set of objectives. They are not merely whimsical preferences or luxuries, but the well researched bases for well-being. On the other hand we are not under any illusions – it will be hard to persuade many people of the need for this shift. For example some recent qualitative research commissioned by nef indicated that many young people see no point in learning for its own sake, that it only has value if it contributes to a career.[3]

So if higher education should prepare people for the good life, how should it be held to account? How can we be sure that it really is delivering this? Perhaps we need to redesign the examinations that it sets and the degrees that it awards so that they also test, reward and demonstrate the skills needed for flourishing, rather than only those needed to secure jobs or increase salaries. In the UK, perhaps The Quality Assurance

---

2   Sir Ken Robinson describes aesthetic experiences as those when your 'senses are operating at their peak', you feel 'fully alive', 'present in the moment' and 'resonating with the excitement of the experience'. He argues that the arts address this idea. See http://www.youtube.com/watch?v=zDZFcDGpL4U for the RSA Animate of his October 2010 talk.

3   Work currently in progress, new economics foundation

Agency for Higher Education (QAA) should ask all institutions to re-apply for degree awarding powers, only passing those that perform well across these new, broader criteria. Perhaps the Higher Education Funding Council for England (HEFCE) needs to adopt well-being criteria comparable to the economic criteria it already uses in its decision making.

Does this seem far-fetched? Remember that the Prime Minister, David Cameron has said:

> "Improving our society's sense of well-being is, I believe, the central political challenge of our times."[4]

David Willetts, Minister of State for Higher Education, has also stated that we need a measure of well-being to rival GDP. If we are incorporating subsidiary objectives into our assessment criteria then why not the main objective?

So the relative ease of measuring economic performance may have given Browne a trump card, but not the ace of trumps. For there is a well-established theory of what is needed to create the good life and there is no good reason why, with an assessment framework that holds HEIs to account, higher education cannot successfully deliver many of its elements in the future.

Charles Seaford is Head of the Centre for Well-being at nef (the new economics foundation) and takes an overview role of all of its work. He is a member of the ONS Advisory Forum on national well-being and was the author of nef's recent report on the economics of housing, One Million Homes.

Laura Stoll is an Assistant Researcher at the Centre for Well-being at nef. She has been researching for the History of Wellbeing project and co-ordinates the All-Party Parliamentary Group on Wellbeing Economics.

nef is a London-based 'think and do tank' founded in 1986. It is unusual in combining rigorous analysis and policy debate with developing practical solutions 'on the ground'. The Centre for Well-being at nef is an award-winning, internationally recognised centre of expertise. It is currently advising the UK Office of National Statistics, the European Union statistical office (Eurostat) and the OECD, and working with the University of Cambridge, Halloran Philanthropies and the Department of Health. It has also published a number of influential reports, notably Measuring our progress: the power of well-being (2011), The (un)Happy Planet Index (2006 and 2009) and National Accounts of Well-being (2009).

---

4   http://news.bbc.co.uk/1/hi/uk_politics/5003314.stm [Accessed 08.04.11]

Louis Coiffait is a Policy Manager within the Pearson Centre for Policy and Learning where he is researching issues such as higher education, enterprise education, STEM skills, education data and careers advice. He tweets and blogs on higher education policy news and analysis at @LouisMMCoiffait and www.pearsoncpl.com/category/HE-policy-blog, is a Fellow of the RSA, a regular volunteer, a school Governor in Hackney and runs the social enterprise Work&Teach in his spare time.

The Pearson Centre for Policy and Learning aims to be a respected voice in education that harnesses the depth and breadth of expertise within Pearson, the world's leading learning company, and key external partners, to provide a range of valuable, original and timely outputs for the sector and for policymakers, on the key issues that matter.

Why contradiction is (and always will be) higher education's great strength

Martin Hughes

Higher education is full of contradiction. Contradiction conjures up images of uncertainty. And that makes me hopeful for the future.

Universities thrive on exploration and multiple perspectives. Every institution is rife with healthy argument. The pursuit of learning often conflicts with the pursuit of a better career. In short, one person's potion is another's poison.

No single purpose for HE can be defined. Yet this is precisely why I am optimistic. Far from a lack of purpose, we should celebrate an abundance of purposes.

However, in such uncertain times, focus can get lost amongst the contradiction. Ferdinand von Prondzynski says:

> *"...students sometimes [see HE] solely as the route to a formal qualification to establish their careers, industry as a way of providing specialist and sometimes quite narrow skills, and governments as a way of keeping people off the dole queues. The educational character of education is sometimes lost in all this and needs to be re-discovered.[1]"*

As a diverse community, we cannot all face the same direction, but we should aim to work as a collective nonetheless. The sector has faced – among other things – an economic crisis, the Browne review, an altered fees system, and a forthcoming White Paper, fuelling uncertainty at the worst possible time. Contradiction can offer a lifeline:

> *"Contradiction... reminds us that resolution is fragile, temporary and, very often, incomplete – that disorder always looms. But perhaps these are the very qualities that fuel an inquiring mind. Perhaps we need contradiction to keep us alert to the responsibility of acting on our imaginations.[2]"*

Our responsibility as individuals and as a collective should still offer flexibility. A broad brush approach to policy should be replaced by arrangements that can focus more

1 "Do students learn anything much at college?", Ferdinand von Prondzynski - http://bit.ly/fOxafN
2 " Working imaginatively with/in contradiction", Journal of Higher Education Policy and Management, 33:2, p.1

specifically on different types of engagement within HE. It is necessary for a sector that has been given too many roles; otherwise focus is increasingly replaced by dilution.

According to outgoing president of Universities UK, Steve Smith:

> *"we must work together as a united sector, celebrating difference, not seeing it as hierarchy, and always celebrating excellence in all its forms[3]".*

There is no doubt that individuals within the sector assume many different identities. This should be applauded, so long as there is scope to work in a capacity that highlights the many, sometimes opposing, strengths of the sector. HE should benefit society as a whole[4]. To do this, focus must rest more on achievement, and less on competition.

However, as public funding is replaced by larger loans, universities (and students) are entering a time of commodification and marketisation. Should institutions seek continued success by covering a growing number of bases, or by choosing to concentrate from a more specialist viewpoint?

In true contradictory terms, I say both. The student landscape is changing and the future of funding is unlikely to be clear any time soon. It is crucial to open doors to an ever-diverse population and to provide accordingly. The trouble is making sense of how to 'provide accordingly'.

Policy-makers are in danger of rushing into inappropriate action at the very time when measured leadership[5] will surely pay the greatest dividends[6]. Those offering creative leadership will seek to capitalise on continuous change, rather than attempting to maintain a rigid set of goals. Change requires agility, not a mad dash.

Until we fully acknowledge the wide remit HE covers, we cannot clearly identify the major (sometimes uniquely defining) differences within. Education as a concept is subjective and covers such varied purposes that universities cannot help but compete "on status rather than educational effectiveness[7]". The future of HE should allow status to be less about false or misleading hierarchies and more about Who, What,

---

3   "Meeting our shared aspirations: Supporting economically and socially relevant higher education", Perspectives 14:3, p.75

4 "System members at odds: managing divergent perspectives in the higher education change process", Kathy Barnett, Journal of Higher Education Policy and Management, 33:2, p.138

5   "Maximising the effectiveness of a scenario planning process", Nicola Sayers, Perspectives 15:1, p.14

6   "Serve the servants, or leadership by degrees", Finbarr Livesey, Times Higher Education, 31 March 2011

7   "Policy Watch", Roger Brown, Perspectives 14:4, p.128

Why, When, Where and How it can boost the needs and desires of society and its members[8].

Therefore, rushed decisions to save money are short-sighted. Stasis needs to be challenged, but so does change. The nature of HE suggests it should keep on questioning, giving and developing in line with our own inquisitiveness as human beings. We objectivise and restrict/limit at our peril!

I am especially impressed by Lincoln's 'Student as Producer'[9], which aims to reconnect research and teaching "in a way that consolidates and substantiates the values of academic life". Students actively engage in research and learning, rather than consuming knowledge. The unique elements at Lincoln are the students, the active research, and the ethos. Focus moves from subjects and qualifications to a way of being. Difference and contradiction are welcomed and – better still – can benefit everyone.

Alternative institutions which aspire to make education completely free and available to everyone, such as Leicester's Third University[10] and the Really Open University[11], should not be seen as competition to other centres of learning. The future of HE will likely include open institutions, just as it will include private providers and corporate-sponsored courses. Alternatives may not currently hand out recognised qualifications or feature in league tables, yet their development may impact wider society just as much as the established universities of today.

It is, therefore, clear that nobody should have a monopoly on education; neither on its purpose, nor on its uses. Removing contradiction only serves to close doors on those who could benefit. Doors need opening, both metaphorically and geographically:

> *"[Study locations] are not fixed, static, or unchanging. We create the locations we study, and this recognition ought to encourage us to continue to remap the geographies of literacy and cultural forms.[12]"*

Global diversity is certain to impact students as much as universities. Applicants will make greater personal choices. Traditional school leavers will not treat university as a 'matter of course'. Considerations will go far beyond[13] gaining a 'good degree'[14].

8   "Towards a pedagogy for a public university", Campaign for the Public University - http://bit.ly/i9KpLD
9   http://studentasproducer.lincoln.ac.uk/
10 http://thirduniversity.wordpress.com/
11 http://reallyopenuniversity.wordpress.com/
12 "Global Matters: The Transnational Turn in Literary Studies", Paul Jay, Cornell University Press, 2010, pp.3-4
13 "English degrees for £27k – who's buying?", John Sutherland, The Guardian, 30 November 2010
14 "Vocational to Higher Education: An International Perspective", Gavin Moodie, Open University

At the same time, we are about to see a steady decline in numbers of 18 to 21 year olds from 2012 onwards. Even in 2010, 35% of students entering HE had no UCAS points[15]. Institutions will be forced to cater to a wider base of people than even today. Many will be unable to study within current frameworks. This is an opportunity for further income, not just extra spending.

Preparation is crucial to allow that income, however. The government are working to make more information available and accessible to prospective students. That work must continue, ongoing, to find ways in which that information can be:

1. Translated into something meaningful so as to allow reasoned choice, rather than increase confusion;

2. Distributed effectively to all groups with the express aim that they will actively engage with the detail.

Reay et al highlight the importance of this:

> *"We found little evidence of the consumer rationalism that predominates in official texts. There were some students who could be described as active researchers... but many relied on serendipity and intuition.[16]"*

Choice will go way beyond the matter of cost. Much of the recent media storm regarding HE revolved around tuition fees, but debate of good and poor value should not start or end with fees. Value will continue to manifest itself in many other ways: Institutions will look increasingly different; outcomes will be more specific to the individual; vocation and employability will form just one aspect of HE.

Therefore, as HE funding goes through change, so do perceptions of HE. For some, education should be a right at every level of learning. For some, education is for training a future workforce. For some, education is about improving society for the better. For some, education makes sure we all have a future.

If we can successfully embrace contradiction and use it to our advantage, I am confident that the future will be worlds apart, and yet remain both startlingly and reassuringly familiar.

Martin Hughes is a writer, specialising in higher education policy and the student experience. He blogs for students at TheUniversityBlog and can be found linking all sorts of HE material via Twitter at @universityboy.

Press, 2008, p.6

15 "Higher Education Supply and Demand to 2020", HEPI, 2011 - http://bit.ly/hGYrtn

16 "Degrees of Choice: Social Class, Race & Gender in Higher Education", Diane Reay, Miriam E. David & Stephen Ball, Trentham Books, 2005, p.159

A worried parent writes

Stefan Stern

"Plumbing college." This was my wife's not entirely satirical answer to the question about where she hoped our children might end up studying. Plumbing college clearly has a lot to recommend it. You learn useful and relevant skills there. You become eminently employable. And you probably don't find yourself having £30,000 of tuition fees to pay back when you finally complete the course.

But all this talk of fees and employability takes us down an avenue I would prefer the debate on higher education could avoid, at least in the first instance. This anxious parent was an undergraduate in the 1980s, a time when certain truths about student life remained self-evident, in spite of the serious economic transformation the UK was going through at the time.

A humanities student in the 1980s, pursuing a non-vocational course, could still feel confident that the degree he or she was studying was worthwhile in itself. University was supposed to be about a broadening and deepening of the individual. The clue was in the name: one hoped to leave having developed a richer understanding of the universe and one's own place in it.

Over the last three decades this notion of higher education as an unquestioned good has begun to slip. It wasn't just Margaret Thatcher but also a Labour Secretary of State for education – a *Labour* Secretary of State – who ruminated out loud on the usefulness of studying medieval history.[1] During this period the fashionable concept of employability became accepted as a key goal – perhaps the key goal – of education. I don't think I am imagining having once heard the then Prime Minister, Tony Blair (a graduate of St. John's College, Oxford), declare, apparently without irony, that;

> *"The more you learn the more you earn."*

But should I now suppress what some might consider to be self-indulgent instincts? Must higher education be seen primarily as a sensible and pragmatic down-payment towards the creation of future earning potential? What advice should the conscientious parent give to his or her children as far as higher education is concerned?

The question of cash cannot be avoided. The great and necessary expansion of university places had to be paid for somehow. Tuition fees – a kind of delayed graduate

---

1   The Guardian (2003) 'Clarke dismisses medieval historians' www.guardian.co.uk/uk/2003/may/09/highereducation.politics

tax – are here to stay, in one form or another. And once the political row and outrage (real and synthetic) have died down, all of us will have to think calmly about how we will help our children cope with the burden of debt they will inevitably incur.

Not unlike the original student loans which came in to replace grants, borrowing to pay back the cost of tuition fees over time will probably turn out to be one of the best and most affordable loans any young person ever takes out. The parents of future students will have to assume the role of financial educators, explaining and reassuring that these debts will prove manageable and will be paid off, in time. It may well also be the case, however, that with the growing downward mobility of much of the 'squeezed middle' in this country, parental (financial) help of the kind I and many others enjoyed as recently as 20-odd years ago will become a much rarer phenomenon.

And that realisation drags me back to a more defiant and uncompromising thought about higher education. Forget future earning potential. Three or more years at university, however they are financed, are an immense privilege. This is not a time to waste, frankly, pursuing a subject or discipline you have no interest in purely because you have an idea that great riches may lie at the other end of that degree. Future doctors must study medicine and future geologists must study geology – that is clear. But what I shall tell my children in due course is that university is there for them to deepen their love of a subject and to develop as individuals. Job prospects, employability skills and building networks of 'contacts', must be a secondary or even tertiary concern. Study something that fascinates you, and worry about the future later on.

Irresponsible advice? I hope not. Education for education's sake? Why not? Medieval history must be endlessly stimulating, and not nearly as useless as the former Secretary of State suggested. Classicists would be able to tell us that Aristotle's concept of 'flourishing' as an individual – *eudaimonia* – does not imply great material success at all. Living and doing well is what matters. One probably needs to be well educated to achieve this, but not necessarily paid an investment banker's salary (or bonus).

Perhaps I will be condemning my children to decades of penury and miserable rented accommodation – or guaranteeing that they never leave home. But if some school teachers are too nervous to speak up for education as a good thing in itself, and academics are too scared or too busy, then someone will have to. It may as well be the parents who take on this lonely but important task. To graduate in the university of life – I mean as a human being, and not merely as an employee or consumer – it may be necessary to do some serious study at a real university first.

Stefan Stern *is a former FT columnist, is now Visiting Professor at Cass Business School, London, and Director of Strategy at Edelman, the PR firm. He has two noisy but highly teachable children.*

British universities past, present and future: convergence and divergence

Robert Anderson

Among the twenty universities in the research-intensive Russell Group, only one (Warwick) is less than 100 years old (http://www.russellgroup.ac.uk). Clearly history still matters. British universities were of diverse origins and types, formed by layers of historical development, but converged over time towards a single model.[1] Uniformity was at its height in the 'Robbins era' from the 1960s to the 1980s, but since then tensions have grown within an ostensibly unified system. Should this fragmentation be deplored, or seen as a natural development to be welcomed and managed? And what are the likely effects on it of a market based around student demand? Should institutions which are central to the life and culture of the nation be shaped purely by competitive forces, or guided along rational paths by the state?

The modern university system was shaped in the 19th century. University models varied, partly geographically, partly functionally. Oxford and Cambridge, themselves radically reformed by the Victorian state, were national universities which formed a governing elite through liberal education. The redbrick universities which developed from the 1870s served local civic communities, and welcomed scientific and vocational subjects. The Scottish universities combined general education with a strong emphasis on professional training. The various colleges which made up the University of London had both civic and national roles, and by the early 20th century had joined Oxbridge to form an academic 'golden triangle'.

Centralisation of academic culture was one of the forces driving convergence. The size and prestige of Oxford and Cambridge made them powerful models. Redbrick universities did not initially have degree powers, and London external degrees provided uniform curricula and standards. From 1889 the state gave annual grants to the new universities in England and Wales (as was already the case in Scotland), and to qualify for these, and for the royal charters which eventually gave degree rights, common standards had to be observed. By 1914, all universities except Oxford and Cambridge relied on the state for up to a third of their funding, and this incipient national system was consolidated by the creation of the University Grants Committee (UGC) in 1919. The UGC distributed state grants while respecting university autonomy, and in the 1920s and 1930s was a conservative force. Traditional conceptions of the university, stressing teaching as much as research, were maintained, and the few new foundations of this period had to wait many years for charters.

---

1   R. Anderson, *British Universities Past and Present* (London, Continuum, 2006).

In 1939 there were 50,000 students in Britain, representing less than two percent of the age group. But expansion began once the war was over, and the UGC became more active. Two key developments in fact preceded the Robbins report of 1963 – the foundation of nine new campus-based universities, of which the first, Sussex, opened in 1961; and the decision in 1962 that the state would pay the fees of all students and give them maintenance grants to study wherever they wished. A jungle of grants and scholarships was swept away. These policies effectively nationalised universities and encouraged them to abandon their local roots. The older civic universities, and even the Scottish ones, now began to build halls of residence, and living in a community was seen as part of the university experience. More significantly, universal entitlement to state funding brought the universities into line with the principles of social justice embodied in the post-war settlement. University education was seen as a public good accessible to all citizens on equal terms. In practice, this civic right was conditioned by many cultural and social factors, not least the exceptional inequalities in British secondary schooling. But meritocracy now extended to Oxbridge, and for forty years needs-blind admission was a reality throughout higher education.

Also in the 1960s, several former 'colleges of advanced technology' were given university status. The Robbins report envisaged that this promotion of local colleges as they matured would continue, but in 1965 the adoption of the 'binary' policy blocked this by diverting expansion into a 'public sector' based on thirty or so polytechnics; no new universities were founded between 1969 and 1992.

Both Robbins and the universal fees policy assumed continuance of selective secondary education, which restricted the numbers qualifying for university entrance and initiated students into academic values. At this time, state grammar schools and independent schools could compete on fairly equal terms. Robbins was about extending and opening up elite university education on meritocratic principles rather than mass higher education, and insisted that expansion should not compromise the quality of the university experience. Since the model, inspired ultimately by Oxbridge, was a residential one with low staff-student ratios, this was an expensive recipe for growth.

In the Robbins era uniformity was at its height. For thirty years, the binary system sheltered universities from wider social pressures, allowing many elite characteristics to be preserved. Research and postgraduate study became more important, giving British universities a high international reputation. They achieved a broad equilibrium between teaching and research, between elite formation and democratic selection, between state funding and university autonomy. But elite assumptions became less plausible as the age participation ratio rose from about 4 per cent in 1962 to 13 per cent - 300,000 students – by 1980.[2]

---

2   W. A. C. Stewart, *Higher Education in Postwar Britain* (Basingstoke, Macmillan), 268, 278.

The public sector also saw convergence as specialist art colleges and colleges of education were merged into polytechnics. But there were tensions within the sector. Some of its leaders proclaimed a 'polytechnic philosophy' celebrating the distinctiveness of these 'people's universities', devoted to teaching rather than research, vocational and practical in their curricula, and at the service of local communities. Yet 'academic drift' brought polytechnics closer to universities, and they were removed from local government control in 1988, blurring the binary frontier.

Its abolition in 1992 might seem to mark further convergence, as old and new universities were integrated. But in fact hierarchies of prestige and quality survived, as the proliferation of 'mission groups' testifies.[3] Differences were widened by an explosion of student demand, driven by underlying social pressures and unanticipated by governments, with numbers more than doubling since 1992 from one to over two million (http://www.hesa.ac.uk). They include far more adult and part-time students, better served by the community traditions of the new universities than by the older model. The political dilemma has been how to reduce per capita expenditure while safeguarding the more prestigious and internationally reputed universities.[4] One answer was to use the Research Assessment Exercise (RAE) to direct funding selectively. Another was variable fees, which were not only politically controversial, but met resistance from a collective university culture hostile to economic competition.

The effects of the RAE overlap with those of globalisation: some universities aim (not always realistically) to compete at 'world class' level and appear in research-based international league tables, while others stress their local status and teaching mission. Yet another issue is the devolution of university policy to Scottish, Welsh and Northern Irish governments. As these continue to resist the English full-fee policy, and to consider their universities as national institutions funded primarily by the state, this divergence is likely to increase.

Advantages already cluster around one group of universities, which combine social prestige, competitive recruitment, access to desirable careers, international reputation, and success in research. The danger is that these universities will become more socially exclusive, as the natural effect of free markets in education is to reproduce existing inequalities of wealth and privilege (http://www.suttontrust.com). Social mobility is an issue governments cannot ignore, and not the only one: universities are complex institutions fundamental to cultural life, economic prosperity, social cohesion and national identity. Mass higher education inevitably brings institutional

---

3   W. Humes, 'Tribalism and competitive branding in (Scottish) higher education', *Scottish Educational Review*, 42 (2010), 3-18.

4   K. Mayhew, C. Deer & M. Dua, 'The move to mass higher education in the UK: many questions and some answers', *Oxford Review of Education*, 30 (2004), 65-82.

diversity, but it needs great faith in markets to believe that student demand alone will produce a rational pattern of functions. The more likely outcome is a pseudo-market manipulated haphazardly from above, which is not obviously preferable to the more coherent university policies pursued in the past, or to the sort of articulated structure found in public systems like that of California. To have a chance of understanding, let alone shaping the future of higher education, we cannot ignore the weight of the past.

Robert Anderson *is Professor Emeritus of History at the University of Edinburgh. He has written extensively on the history of universities.*

Section three – How should higher education be delivered?

Diversity in higher education and social mobility

Matt Grist and Julia Margo

Let us introduce you to Asa (not her real name). We met Asa at a Community College in Hackney. Asa was a 'learning advocate', someone who represents the college to external visitors like us, and who observes lessons, carries out research and advocates on behalf of students to the college's senior staff. Asa was a bright, focussed young woman. And she wanted to go to university.

What she wanted to study was radiography. She told us how her mother had died of cancer when she was nine years-old, and how her best friend had died of leukaemia two years ago. She wanted to study radiography to help people like her mother and her friend. And she wanted to study near to her home so that she could continue to live with her family. She also wanted to get her degree as quickly as possible so she could enter the workplace.

As debates rage around tuition fees and the role of universities in promoting social mobility, we might ask ourselves whether higher education serves people like Asa well? The answer seems to be an overwhelming no. Not only have university places – as is well documented now – been captured on the whole by the middle classes,[1] but the very idea of what it means to participate in higher education has become a middle class shibboleth. The idea goes something like this: leave home and explore yourself through study, extra-curricular activities and revelry; meet a circle of friends with whom you'll make the transition into stable, well-rewarded and connected professional careers; get drunk with those university friends and possibly marry one of them.

This vision is not one that appealed to Asa, and it does not appeal to many other young people, especially those forced to grow up a little faster than their more affluent peers. Asa does not need to make the transition to adulthood through an elongated finishing school with occasional bouts of studying in between, nor does she need to explore herself. She knows who she is and she knows what she wants to do. She simply needs a higher education system and a labour market that enables her to do it.

1   In 1960 the percentage of first year undergraduates from middle-class backgrounds was 74%, it was exactly the same in 1999 even though the size of the yearly cohort had increased massively. See Wolf, Alison: *Does Education Matter,* Penguin, 2002.

There are three policy ideas that would make the higher education system better serve young people like Asa in the future: the liberalisation of degree-awarding institutions; more variety in the length of university degrees; and employment regulations that outlaw unnecessary discrimination on the basis of levels of educational attainment. Now, briefly, to each of these in turn.

At the moment, it takes an act of Parliament or a Royal Charter to visit degree-awarding powers on a new institution. This level of oversight might at first seem unnecessarily draconian, but there is reason to it. Universities are guardians of learning and culture, and their 'brand' should not be damaged by too many unwarranted entrants into the market. However, some more flexibility could be introduced into the system such that Further Education (FE) colleges could be allowed to carry out teaching and assessment towards degrees under patronage from a local university. This already happens to some extent with foundation degrees through franchising and accreditation arrangements, and there is no reason in principle why it should not be extended to full degrees, as long as standards are maintained through all the usual channels, most notably the use of external examiners. The marker of higher education is not physical location in a university, but studying something to a certain level of depth and breadth, and under one's own steam, so that a degree signals a particular standard of education.

As for more variety in the length of degrees, in the USA and Canada it is common for students to finish degrees a year or so quicker than is standard by taking summer classes (often taught by PhD students or visiting academics). In the UK, the university of Buckingham (a private university), offers degrees that can be finished in two years. These are not just 'vocational' degrees like the one Asa wants to take, but arts and humanities degrees too. The brevity of study is achieved through studying all year round, with shorter holidays. No less material need be covered since the average university 'year' in the UK is one hundred days, leaving plenty of scope for gains in efficiency.

The main stumbling block to expanding the offer of shorter degrees is the culture of universities – long holidays and sabbaticals for academics to carry out research. But this culture is itself damaging since it homogenises academics into researcher/teacher hybrids. Some are suited to this role but not all. The result is not just the bog-standard length of a degree, but also many researchers who teach badly and many teachers who carry out questionable research. All this produces a massive inefficiency in the system. With liberalised degree-awarding institutions, based on a partnership model, there would be jobs for those academics better suited to teaching (and doing it all year round), as well as for those better at research, who would be freed up to do just that, giving less frequent lectures. This division of labour would have to be based on academic merit and would meet with some resistance from the academic community. But it would only be recognising differences in talent that already exist and it would increase the quality of universities (better teaching, better research), as well as creating efficiency gains.

Finally, to the supply-side issue of legislating against unnecessary demands for possession of qualifications. It seems odd to claim more regulation could free up people's ability to gain wages for their labour. But there is a wealth of evidence now that the UK is over-educating for many jobs(estimates range between a quarter and a third of the workforce being over-educated).[2] All that we suggest here is that it be possible for an applicant to question at tribunal the legitimacy of making demands for qualifications when advertising jobs. If, for example, an applicant challenged a chartered accountancy firm for demanding chartered accountant exams, then this would cut little ice at a tribunal. But if a local council is advertising a clerical post and demands a university degree (which does happen), then applicants should be able to go to tribunal to demand the employer display evidence of why such a qualification is necessary. In this case, the employer would be on much shakier ground. For people like Asa, who might consider a foundation degree plus a real willingness to learn on the job plenty good enough to become a radiographer, an employer might find it difficult to justify *demanding* a full degree. In reality, of course, regulations of this kind would lead to lots of job applications simply being reworded with phrases like 'a degree is desirable' but this shift in tone would be no small victory against pointless over-education.

With these policy reforms in place, Asa would have much more choice of local providers of a full degree; could get her degree in a shorter time, saving considerable costs and satisfying her desire to enter the labour market as soon as possible; and would be less-likely to be forced to over-educate herself to pursue her chosen career.

What we need to ask ourselves is why our higher education and labour market don't serve people like Asa as well as they could? The argument that by taking a shorter more local degree Asa is entering the lesser part of a 'two-tier' system doesn't hold water. If Asa wanted to take a longer degree or leave home she could; the point is she doesn't. Are we to ascribe, patronisingly, false consciousness to her? Or admit that we have suffused our idea of a university education with notions of the rites of passage of the middle-classes? With more diversity in the university sector and a labour market less insistent on over-education, more people would have more options for social mobility than they currently have. That's liberal politics spreading opportunity, not regressive elitism.

---

2   See Chevalier, A. and Lindley, J. (2009) Over-education and the Skills of UK graduates Journal of the Royal Statistical Society 172.2

Dr Matt Grist is a Senior Researcher on the Family and Society Programme at Demos. His expert areas include education (including vocational education), capabilities, social mobility, youth policy and behaviour change.

Julia Margo is Deputy Director at Demos. Julia is a regular commentator in the international and national press. She also writes for national, online and specialist press and is an experienced chair and public speaker on a wide range of subjects.

Demos is a think-tank focused on power and politics. Our unique approach challenges the traditional, 'ivory tower' model of policymaking by giving a voice to people and communities. We work together with the groups and individuals who are the focus of our research, including them in citizens' juries, deliberative workshops, focus groups and ethnographic research.

Institutional values and the student experience

Annie Gosling and Owen Gower

Who cares what the institutional structures of a university are, provided that the best student educational opportunities are preserved? Well, it may be that bureaucratic and financial structures are not isolable from the intellectual development of students. Will students have a different – worse? – educational experience if their university is privately run, or if they get a degree in two years rather than three, or if the delivery of their degree is out-sourced to further education (FE) colleges? In what follows we discuss these three institutional developments and consider their potential impact on the educational experience of students.

Alternative private providers

Government will widen opportunities for private institutions to take over some of the educational role of universities. Students at private universities will have access to the same Government sponsored loans and grants. In addition Government will give more degree-awarding powers to private education institutions. There is nothing to stop these privately run institutions from having a research agenda. But if research council money is tied to public universities, then private research opportunities will be limited. If so, it is likely that private universities will focus on teaching, and not – in the main – on research. What implications might this have for the student experience?

If the pressure to research is lessened, it may follow that the quality of teaching will rise. The reputation for delivering a satisfactory learning environment will no doubt become a key market driver. So, private universities may be more attentive to teaching standards than universities have been – so much the better for the student experience.

Except, of course, that the learner may not be the best judge of whether their learning environment is satisfactory. Poor communication skills and late, indecipherable marking are clear indications of an unsatisfactory educational experience, but other indicators are vexed. Some subjects are painful to learn, but it would be a pity to exclude them from the syllabus because pain is usually unsatisfactory. Marks and results ought also to be somewhat insulated from the satisfaction of the learner.

Will an educational market driven by student-consumers find itself beholden to satisfaction ratings? Perhaps not, if – as some optimists suggest – students are discriminating enough consumers to recognise that grade inflation and syllabus distortions will bring the very status of being a graduate into disrepute.

Outsourcing teaching

Another suggestion made has been to separate degree-awarding powers from teaching. Local institutions such as further education colleges would teach students locally but their degree would be awarded by a university. Potentially students could study at a local institution, be taught by local staff but achieve a degree from a prestigious university. This would enable people the opportunity to access higher education who may not be free to move due to community ties, caring responsibilities or financial constraints. Clearly though, the corporate life of the university would be absent under this arrangement. Does that affect the educational experience? Satellite learning may give the impression that active epistemic practices need not be internalised. The practices being taught may remain remote, not done by the tutors and therefore not to be attempted by the student.

Three years to two

Rather than degree study taking the traditional three years, courses could be completed in two by increasing the length of terms. This is partly possible because those teaching them will not be required to conduct and publish research. Efficiency savings ensue: University campuses would no be longer unused for half the year. It also means savings for the students who will only need to find the money to pay for two years' worth of accommodation, living expenses and fees. They will also be able to enter the job market sooner and more conditioned to the intensity of a workplace routine.

Paradoxically, though graduates will be used to professional routines they will have had less opportunity to experience work. The majority of students devote at least part of their holidays to gaining work experience, knowledge of the 'real world' they are continually told is vital if they want to get a job after graduation. Will this opportunity exist within a packed two year programme? Does it offer different and valuable 'tasters' of work compared to a full career job?

Beside this is another more philosophical concern about compressed learning. Being so intensely immersed in the routine of the degree subject will entail the crowding out of wider issues. It may be for example that the academic pace discourages students from taking up optional courses out of intellectual curiosity. Active membership of a society or campaigning organisation might require more time than these students can afford to give.

Institutional values and the individual

Three of the institutional values that have traditionally structured universities and are potentially threatened by these developments are: *disinterestedness* – that criticism of ideas, actions and judgements should be conducted selflessly; *communalism* – the idea that knowledge is a product of social collaboration and belongs to the community; and *organised scepticism* – meaning that all ideas, without exception, are subject to systematic analysis and testing. Do these values affect the student educational experience and do the proposed developments in higher education affect these institutional values?

As higher education becomes increasingly consumer driven, disinterested intellectual curiosity is made increasingly vulnerable to extrinsic biases such as student satisfaction or 'employability'. So what? These outcomes are clearly vital but they must not diminish the opportunity for intellectual curiosity. If the marketplace is allowed to define the value of education predominantly by employability or even by student satisfaction, intellectual curiosity could be crowded out. This vulnerability is likely to be more pronounced among private providers who are more susceptible to the vicissitudes of consumer demand.

If satellite education providers lack the 'corporate life' of traditional universities then they lack the means by which to show that knowledge is a product of social collaboration with community ownership. The intellectual autonomy of the learner necessarily suffers if they are only engaged passively and without this sense of ownership. The result is a student without a sense of knowledge as being dynamic and collaborative. Instead knowledge becomes reified and if that happens, the student will be correspondingly disempowered.

Compressing three years of education into two might mean that the fundamental assumptions and implications of student's studies would be unquestioned in the race to the final exam. The danger then becomes that instead of fostering unshackled thinking, universities will turn out overspecialised, gullible graduates unable to respond innovatively to the unforeseen challenges of work and life.

These are, of course, potential threats only. The underlying point is that institutional values – what universities stand for – do affect the student's educational experience. So institutional changes must be made in full cognisance of the implications they will have for the individual student experience.

Annie Gosling is the King George VI Fellow at Cumberland Lodge and a PhD student at Liverpool John Moores University. She is writing her thesis on young people's career aspirations and expectations.

Dr Owen Gower *is a Senior Fellow at Cumberland Lodge and a Visiting Tutor in Philosophy at Royal Holloway and King's College London.*

<u>Cumberland Lodge</u> *is an educational charity in Windsor Great Park. Since 1947 it has been a forum in which university students from a range of disciplines have come to stay for short periods of time. The Lodge provides a space where students can examine the fundamental assumptions and implications of their degree subject as well as how it relates to wider ethical issues.*

What should the college contribution be?

Gareth Parry

Further education (FE) colleges have long been providers of higher education in England. Today, they are seen by government as a cost-effective way of providing higher education and, along with private providers, as a necessary source of competition in a student-led funding regime and market for undergraduate places. This is one of at least four roles that governments have sought for colleges over the last quarter century.

A long perspective is a rare thing in contemporary policymaking. So, here is a tutorial to recover the policy memory and inject some large questions into present-day debates. What the college contribution should be is a question being asked or re-asked in other countries, although a policy interest in the international evidence is not conspicuous. Anyhow, what about the English and their attempts to decide on these matters?

Relieved of responsibility

Before the dramatic expansion that brought mass levels of participation, the policy imperative had been to concentrate higher education in the strongest institutions: the then polytechnics and, on the other side of the binary line, the universities. Legislation in 1988 and 1992 finally allocated institutions of higher education to one sector and further education colleges to another. Any higher level work remaining in the colleges was officially declared residual and, if anything, expected to fall away.

That colleges should not normally do higher education was the first of the positions assumed for further education establishments in the modern era. This broke with the idea of a seamless pattern of further and higher education overseen by local government. Relieved of responsibility for higher education, the primary job of colleges was the education of adults and young people at the lower levels. Once established in their own sector, the college interest in higher education would be a qualifying one (equipping students with entry qualifications), not a providing one.

A special mission

While a two-sector structure of higher education and further education has remained, the policy of keeping colleges away from higher education was soon abandoned. When separated from the polytechnics, most colleges managed to keep their courses of higher education. Generally, these represented small amounts of provision, leading to short-cycle vocational qualifications and catering for part-time students living or working locally. Even so, the college share of higher education was not inconsiderable, at between ten and fifteen per cent of the undergraduate population.

In a reversal of policy, the newly elected Blair government accepted a key recommendation of the Dearing inquiry into higher education. This proposed a special mission for further education colleges at levels below the bachelor degree, with these institutions leading the renewed expansion in undergraduate education which the introduction of tuition fees would help to fund.

The Dearing recommendation insisted on direct funding for colleges to perform this role. Not for Dearing the sinfulness of franchising, the way that a number of colleges had increased their teaching of higher education courses during the expansion years. Over time, colleges would become the primary providers of sub-bachelor qualifications, similar to in Scotland.

Semi-compulsory collaboration

Although adopted, the Dearing recommendation did not survive for long. Concerned about the weak demand for existing sub-degree qualifications, the government invented a new short-cycle qualification, the work-focused Foundation Degree. In partnership with universities and employers, colleges were to be centrally involved in its 'delivery'. Contrary to Dearing, the preferred model for its teaching by colleges was through indirect funding arrangements with partner universities.

In addition to funded student numbers, collaboration brought the award of a university qualification, the responsibility for quality assurance and the guarantee of progression to a bachelor degree. However, such arrangements occasioned insecurity and dependency, whether in the setting of fees or the planning of programmes. This third role for colleges in higher education has come under severe pressure in recent years, with some universities withdrawing their numbers in response to reductions in their public funding.

The next experiment

The post-Dearing settlement has since been replaced by the post-Browne experiment and, with it, another new context and role for further education institutions. Fee differentiation and a de-regulation of awarding powers will, it is ventured, afford colleges more scope to demonstrate their claims to responsiveness, distinctiveness and affordability. At the same time, established sub-degree qualifications like the Higher National Diploma (HND) and Certificate (HNC) are back in the fold, as staged awards and routes to the bachelor degree.

In this fourth phase, the college contribution is to be shaped by the demands of competition, with fewer barriers for institutions that do not currently receive direct funding and with non-teaching organisations able to offer external degrees. Rather than increase the number of institutions with degree-awarding powers, as in the opportunity for colleges to award the Foundation Degree, the interests of students and the system would be better served, it is argued, by colleges teaching towards internationally respected external degrees.

An open system of universities and colleges

With four competing versions on show over twenty-five years, why has it been so difficult to achieve consistency, coherence or consensus on the college contribution to higher education? One major explanation is structural. In a two-sector system, there has been no central authority – a tertiary intelligence – to offer overarching leadership and coordination. Instead, responsibility for higher education in the further education sector has been passed to a body – the Higher Education Funding Council for England (HEFCE) – whose primary constituency is the higher education sector and its member institutions. As an internal HEFCE review came close to saying, the college role in higher education has for long been a source of policy weakness, if not failure.

Nor would a shift of responsibility to the other sector be likely to improve matters, although the experience of Scotland is again instructive where higher education below the bachelor degree is a near-monopoly for the colleges and where the universities have not exercised a direct influence on its shape and development. Scotland now has a single funding council for further and higher education but this is still some distance from the tertiary commission and lifelong learning system that some had imagined for that country.

On one reading, the market-led reforms intended for English higher education invite their extension into the rest of the tertiary system. Whatever their reach, the rationale and architecture of a two-sector system will continue to be challenged. The asymmetries of power and influence inscribed in these structures are one set of reasons for their survival, with higher education able to argue persuasively for separate or special treatment and further education ever-conscious of its subordinate status and confused identity. The time has come perhaps to dump the language of further education and, instead, invest in the concept of an open system of universities and colleges.

Gareth Parry is Professor of Education and Director of the Centre for the Study of Higher Education and Lifelong Learning at the University of Sheffield.

Future access to HE: a view from an 'Independent/ State School Partnership'

Peter Rawling

In 2007 seven schools got together to form an Independent/State School Partnership (ISSP) in the Thames Valley area. The primary aims of the partnership were to raise attainment at GCSE and to raise aspirations to stay on in education at both post-16 and post-18 levels. Three of the schools already had large Sixth Forms and considerable experience of getting students into higher education, others were developing Sixth Forms and entering the UCAS process for the first time. A Higher Education group was formed to share good practice and to co-ordinate work where appropriate.

What became clear early on was that there was no lack of ambition among the students to do well at school, nor lack of readiness to work hard to achieve results. What was often lacking however was confidence. Many, who had no experience of further education or higher education in their family, doubted that university was "for the likes of them". If that attitude could be dispelled, then the sights were set very locally and the location of courses was often considered to be more important than their content. When confidence and self-esteem are not high, any further impediments that seem to get put in the way have a wholly disproportionate effect. Groups of Year 10s, 11s and Year 12s were addressed immediately after the 2010 announcement of increased university fees. In the schools that had a tradition of university entry it was found that respectively 36%, 40% and 50% felt that they were "significantly put off" the idea of going to university due to the cost and fear of the debt that would follow. "Significantly put off" was defined to the groups as representing a serious doubt that they would now pursue the university route. In the schools that had less of a tradition the figures were even higher.

These views are likely to be replicated among parents. This will be particularly true of the parents of girls in some communities and among families and groups where the potential benefits of degree level education for future employment are less known or understood. These communities can now include even those in affluent areas, who are already seeing a great deal of post-graduate unemployment. In these latter cases the increasing view will be that only degrees from certain universities will be "worth it" and in the former communities that none will. One of the reasons why there is such an imbalance between independent and state-school educated students getting into Russell group universities is that so fewer of the latter apply there in the first place. That imbalance is likely to get even worse unless very direct action is taken. If it isn't, government is likely, and has already begun to some extent, to demand the sort of positive discrimination that will be anathema to the university establishment. We must all do more to try to redress the balance but that task will be made all the harder when the prospect for some families will appear to be a level of anticipated debt that exceeds their annual incomes two or even three-fold.

It needs to be made very clear to both students and their families that the cost to them of future university degrees need not be what the media hype and sensationalist headlines suggest. Nothing needs to be paid up front now, not even the £3,290 currently expected of students as a contribution to fees. A higher level of salary than at present needs to be earned by graduates before repayments begin and even then those repayments will be made at rates below those currently being paid. A lot of potential students will therefore actually be better off under the new scheme than at present.

Universities themselves need to be far more up front about grants, scholarships and bursaries that they offer and more needs to be done to attract donors to create more of them. A double tax break from government for those prepared to set up those awards at universities would greatly encourage the levels of endowment that are seen as the norm in the United States. Such schemes as those where universities become the hub not just of tertiary education but of secondary education in their areas should be encouraged. This would particularly attune students to the nature and quality of universities from early on in their education and help them to see university as a natural progression. All secondary schools need to have a nominated Higher Education liaison officer, who takes responsibility within school for sowing the seeds of aspiration to university as early as possible – certainly before students start to choose their GCSE courses in Year 9. Very few schools presently have such a person other than the Head of Sixth Form, who must wear several hats and puts information across at a stage that is often too late. The Connexions Service, offering advice on careers and HE, will soon no longer exist in many areas and Aim Higher is ending shortly too. HE liaison officers will serve a vital role if applications, and realistic ones, from state schools are to be maintained, let alone increased.

All of this has to be enabled by government. Penalising universities if they don't meet certain arbitrary quotas will be less helpful than positive incentives and taking actions to assist schools in promoting awareness and encouraging ambition. The current climate does not encourage co-operation between schools so partnerships such as ours are less likely to occur in the future to the disadvantage of all concerned in many ways, and certainly in promoting the value of higher education. Partnerships of schools need to be served by universities for whom widening participation is a genuine, and not just a token, aim. They and government could sponsor or subsidise a HE liaison officer in every local authority for far less cost than is currently spent on some schemes that often seem totally cosmetic. We may no longer believe that a 50% rate of progression to university is a realistic, or even desirable, aim but it is the view of the schools in this partnership that every student has an entitlement to aspire to realistic goals. These include higher education, where appropriate, and without further barriers being put in the way of it than those very real challenges that already exist. All parties claim that they wish to see wider participation but they cannot achieve that, if all they do is wish for the 'end' without doing more to enable the 'means'.

Peter Rawling is Deputy Head of The Windsor Boys School and for over thirty years has co-ordinated the Higher Education work there. Since 2007 he has chaired the Partnership's Higher Education group.

In 2007 the **Thames Valley Independent State School Partnership** *was formed between seven schools in the area. These comprised Eton College, Heston Community School in West London, four schools in Slough (Slough and Eton Business and Enterprise College, St. Joseph's Catholic High School, Beechwood School and The Langley Academy) and The Windsor Boys' School. Much has been achieved via this collaboration and all of the schools have pled ged funding and time to continue this co-operation after the official life of the Partnership comes to an end in the summer of 2011.*

How university hinterlands can drive progression

Sue Betts and Kate Burrell

Linking London has been working as a partnership in the permeable area between higher and further education, 'the university and college hinterland[1]' for five years. We have worked collaboratively with as many as thirty five London higher and further education partners, to bring 'clarity, coherence and certainty of progression' to vocational learners. It sounds like a relatively straightforward proposition, to afford the vocational learner a similar expectation and clarity of progression that learners following the more traditional A-level route have enjoyed, the reality is a little different.

Linking London has developed an independent and objective overview of 'progression issues', in a way that organisations working directly on them, we would argue, rarely achieve. In fact it is only recently that the concept of progression has started to enter the discourse of further and higher education as a key success factor. For those people who don't work in education, the issue of moving onwards (for those who have the capacity to benefit) must seem like a fairly straightforward enterprise, unfortunately there are a number of factors in the world of vocational education that do not make this easy. The vocational qualifications themselves are not understood by most people, some are constantly being experimented with (remember GNVQs, Vocational A-levels and the new Diplomas?), and the sectors within education often fail to look beyond their own engagement, either in terms of receiving or progressing students.

What is required is a degree of sophistication and understanding within the world of education and of the people who control, administer, and teach in it. It also requires that programme and curriculum designers think beyond and prior to their own programme and also into (and out of) the labour market[2]. This type of activity begs collaborative endeavour and the development of mutual understanding and agreement[3].

The fact that most vocational learners tend to come from more disadvantaged and socially deprived sections of our communities, or in some instances have found the traditional model of academic learning uninspiring, further compounds the issue of progression. The deficit model that has been developed to 'deal' with these problems

---

1   Hinterland – the land, often remote or undeveloped, that lies behind a coast, the banks of a river, or a folded mountain range. The region lying inland from and served by a port. The region near to, and dependent on, a commercial centre, (from the German *hinter*, behind + *land*, land)

2   The UK Commission for Employment and Skills (UKCES) produces reports and publications on, amongst other topics, the changing skills demands of the nation and how potential learners move into and out of the labour market.

3   Which is the reason why HEFCE funded thirty Lifelong Learning Networks across the country in 2006.

has not been to 'penalise' the course developers for their failure, but, rather to treat the progressing student as somehow lacking the 'tools' to deal with higher education. Tools for learning that surely should have been nurtured far earlier in a learners' education. In response to this assumed deficit, we have seen the emergence of 'bridging' modules and what we in Linking London call the 'sticking plaster' approach to progression.

In our experience at the transition between level three learning (A levels, BTEC Nationals etc) and HE there has been a tremendous blurring of issues to do with pedagogy and the so called distinction between the traditional academic model of A-levels and vocational learning. Good pedagogy should not just be the preserve of the vocational educator; anymore than giving 'disaffected' learners practical work to 'keep them occupied' is an aspiring outcome. Likewise, English universities are rightly celebrated for doing many things right and competing on the world stage in research. We ask that the same passion and innovative approach be applied to teaching and learning, to create flexible pedagogies which can be used to inspire students with diverse educational experiences.

The lack of requisite knowledge, in order to progress, is a separate issue[4] although it is interesting that progression in some areas like Psychology require no matriculation at level three. We would also argue that the imparting of knowledge was possibly a role for education in the past and that now it is surely much more about developing new insights and providing the environment in which learners can interpret, analyse and extrapolate. The task facing admissions tutors is to recognise the 'potential' to succeed in higher learning. Better use of contextual data will prove increasingly important here.

In the Linking London publication, 'The Progression Story[5]' we contend that in order to make progression work (school/FE/HE or employment) an empowered progression champion of sufficient seniority is needed to achieve strategic commitment and operational buy-in. We could argue for 'progression' to be written into all educators' Key Performance Indicators within an institution committed to moving their learners on, either upwards or sideways. Likewise an understanding of what 'progression' means and what 'vocational qualifications' are, should be included in teacher and lecturer training and continuous professional development (CPD).

So, what will future pioneers working in the hinterland see, as we move to greater marketisation and diversification of the English education system? The forthcoming debate on Access Agreements for higher education in the light of higher fees sits on

---

4   As is satisfactory attainment of GCSE maths and English.

5   'The Progression Story' (Betts and Burrell, 2011)

the fine dividing line between outreach for the improvement of social mobility and the competitive demands of recruitment and selection. This requires us to remember the purpose of education and how at its core it must retain its integrity. Institutional mission, corporate and social responsibility, and improving one's contribution to eco-sustainability are all things we expect from good businesses. How important is it to expect them from institutions that educate our current and future generations? With the likelihood of many universities charging the maximum tuition fees, what will students' expectations of their 'university' days entail? HE will have to take note of other consumerist industries and manage their students' expectations carefully. They will also need to articulate clearly the expectations universities will have of students, manifest in their student or learner 'charters'. Traditionally vocational learners are used to a more interactive and negotiated style of learning and teaching, and they may find it easier to succeed in an active learning role, more so perhaps than those who have followed the classic A-level route. Confronted with larger debt, students will make decisions about the 'value' of their qualification in the world of work. Flexible, part-time provision and vocational education routes, which enable learners to 'earn and learn', may become more attractive than three years of full time study. It may be that the time for vocational learning has arrived.

If anything, the terrain in future will be more not less volatile. We should not forget why we are in education and to constantly question and challenge where the market takes us, which is linked to fundamental purposes and long term goals. We know educated societies are happier, less crime ridden and more prosperous places, where people live longer healthier lives. A greater appreciation of, and partnership with, the rich and varied hinterland around each HEI is the best way of improving learner progression.

Sue Betts, the Director of Linking London, *is an educationalist with a long and varied career. A former Vice Principal, she had responsibility for curriculum, staff development and higher education in the Further Education Sector. She has worked for a National Awarding Body, two national distributed e-learning organisations, and as a consultant. As Director, Sue is responsible for the strategic direction of Linking London.*

Dr Kate Burrell is an experienced project manager with a background in teaching, cell biology and neuroscience. More recently her work on partnership and business development in Linking London has included relationship building, brokering progression agreements as well as joint authoring a number of practical reports and publications.

Linking London is a unique network of education partners and stakeholders including small adult-focused organisations through to large multi-purpose further education colleges and highly prestigious research intensive universities, jointly funded by the Higher Education Funding Council for England (HEFCE) and subscriptions from partners. Hosted by Birkbeck, University of London, it was set up in 2006 to improve and create opportunities for vocational learners who want to progress into and through higher education.

HE in FE: renaissance or reformation?

Nick Davy

In the UK, higher education (HE) courses delivered by further education (FE) providers such as colleges, are presently under the spotlight as the Coalition Government grapple with the complexities of creating a more market-orientated higher education system. Speculation about the likely contents of the delayed HE White Paper is the bread and butter conversation of many a conference lunch break.

However, perhaps much of this frenzied focus and speculation about the costs and structure of undergraduate general education is actually a bit of a sideshow, in comparison to the HE needs of the majority of those in the workplace and those who do not want a traditional HE experience. The important priorities for both the economy and individuals are not an expansion of three-year undergraduate degrees, but the need to improve workplace learning, increase apprenticeships at all levels, and up-skill the workforce.[1] There is now an emerging global questioning of the costs and worth of mass three or four year undergraduate education, not just triggered by the recent 'banking recession'. 'Traditional HE' – the three/four year honours degree – based in a university or equivalent organisation, has now become the norm in developed countries for a range of occupational areas and subjects.

A mass HE system has only been in place in England for the past fifteen years, and possibly it is only after this recent experience that we can begin to evaluate its worth against a range of social, economic and cultural indicators. This is not just a theoretical evaluation as some of the c. £6 billion spent by HEFCE each year could be spent on other public goods, or other parts of the education system – early years education for example.

This does not have to be a crude cost-benefit analysis but an honest appraisal of how efficient (inputs/outputs) a mass HE system is in *helping*, for example, to meet key cross-party policy aims such as educating and training people for a more competitive and global future, and improving social mobility. And no, *some* of the university sector cannot simply argue university education is a 'public good' and then evade its widening participation role. In short, could other educational measures be more cost-effective and efficient in achieving these aims?

---

1   HM Treasury (2006) *Leitch Review of Skills: Prosperity for all in the global economy – world class skills*, Final Report. HM Treasury, London

We know that in the UK about 6 million people in work have some form of Level Three qualification; and that the UK still lags behind Germany, France and the USA in productivity.[2] There is also, mainly anecdotal, evidence that more UK graduates are actually progressing to lower-level vocational qualifications post-graduation. In Australia, more graduates now progress from HE to FE than from FE to HE. We also know that achievement of Level Three qualifications, including apprenticeships, lead to higher lifetime earnings on average; and only better returns for *some* graduates, dependent on subject and institution. However;

> *"we must avoid previous policy mistakes that tended to focus on qualification acquisition as an end in itself without recognising the need to bring about genuine improvements in skills levels.[3]"*

So, how do we develop the necessary higher-level vocational and cognitive skills needed for a world that will demand lifelong connections with learning, without an over-emphasis on qualification accumulation?

Firstly, traditional HE is a good thing for the individual and society – graduates tend to earn more, are healthier and add more to civil society.[4] However, traditional HE is expensive in its present form, is about to get more so, and probably inappropriate for some for a variety of reasons – social, economic or 'the wrong time'. Moreover, studying for a degree in History or English literature does not mean you will develop appropriate, work-ready 'employability skills'; that is not what that type of degree gives you.

What we need is a diverse HE system, including traditional HE, but also featuring credible alternatives such as higher apprenticeships and shorter, HE-equivalent periods of study, focussed on skill development both at college/university and in the workplace. This could include expanding the accreditation of in-house company training schemes, more recognition and accreditation of prior experience and knowledge, accelerated learning programmes, and more learning delivered and assessed in the workplace.[5]

2   UKCESa (2011) *Review of Employment and Skills*. UKCES. London

3   BIS (2011) Social Mobility: A Literature Review. BIS London

4   Feinstein, L., Budge, D., Vorhaus, J. and Duckworth, K. (2008) *The social and personal benefits of learning: A summary of key research findings*. London, Centre for Research on the Wider Benefits of Learning, Institute of Education. London

5   UKCESb (2011) *The UK Employment and Skills Almanac 2010 Evidence Report 26*. UKCES. London

Secondly, Government needs to set the overall policy direction with a transfer of funds from the traditional HE market to the proposed, more diverse model, funded partly from the loan book. Others will need to play their part; employers becoming more innovative in their recruitment and CPD practices; schools/colleges improving their careers guidance, and sector skills councils introducing career and learning pathways such as those developed by the Sector Skills Councils (SSCs) Cogent and Lantra. The Universities & Colleges Admissions Service (UCAS) will also need to adapt. And the more prestigious universities need to stop complaining about their fairly benign widening participation targets and meet them in full, otherwise loan funding should be withdrawn.

So yes, the unthinkable – a reduction in traditional HE student numbers, but an expansion in a variety of other forms of HE and a re-framing of what 'higher education' means.

Unfortunately, at present this seems to be exactly what will not happen. Private providers are set to continue supplying 'cheap to deliver', bog-standard, traditional HE, in already over-supplied subject areas such as business studies and law, and even the spectre of 'liberal arts colleges' has surfaced.[6]

These entrants may pressurise the newer universities to re-examine their costs and prices, possibly no bad thing, but they will do nothing to address the wider higher-level vocational skills needs for sectors such as engineering, construction and pharmaceuticals – and others – or the UK productivity gap.

Last, there is little point in spending several million pounds in transactional costs to create some form of HE quasi-market if the end result is more of the same, because that is not what the economy or our society needs.

What is needed is traditional HE, probably at a lower price and with tough widening participation targets, and a flexible, consumer and employer-led 'other system' – equally funded – that focuses on higher level skills development, part-time and blended provision, and credited learning in the workplace. And that vision can only be achieved by organisations such as FE colleges, working in partnership with HE institutions, rooted in their local communities and with strong links to local and regional employers. And over time hopefully featuring a proper HE credit accumulation and transfer system that includes individual learning accounts. So what is the future for

---

6   Willetts D speech to UUK Annual Conference 25th February 2011 http://www.bis.gov.uk/news/speeches/david-willetts-uuk-spring-conference-2011 [Accessed 14.04.11]

HE? It's not clear, but if we're brave enough it should be a genuinely new role for FE, as Watson puts it:

> "The flexibility which a proper credit framework brings will be needed all the more in the light of current economic turbulence… this is not a technical issue: we have the systems. It is a cultural and moral issue: we fail to use these systems for reasons of conservatism, snobbery and lack of imagination.[7]"

Nick Davy is the Higher Education Policy Manager at the Association of Colleges (AoC).

Association of Colleges (AoC) exists to represent and promote the interests of Colleges and provide members with professional support services.

---

7   Watson (2009) *Lifelong Learning and the Future of Higher Education; IFLL Sector Paper 8.* NIACE. Leicester

Section four – How should we make the most of technology and data?

Seizing the opportunity for online learning

Lynne Brindley

The importance of online learning was recognised by the Higher Education Funding Council for England (HEFCE) which set up a Task Force in September 2009 to consider the opportunities for UK universities both nationally and internationally. I was privileged to chair the Task Force and this short personal piece reflects on that work, which formally concluded in January 2011 with the report referenced below[1]. I have picked out some of the major recurring issues, the golden threads running through the report and the broad trends underlying the future opportunities for online learning.

Throughout our work we aimed to keep the student as learner at the centre of our deliberations. What is extremely clear is that the developing needs and expectations of students are rapidly changing and that generally they see online learning through technology as enhancing their choices and, if properly implemented, enhancing the quality of their higher education experience.

They do not perceive the use of ICT in learning as a 'second-rate' alternative, nor is it seen as a substitute for quality face-to-face interactions with academics and their peers. Time and time again students were adamant that excellence is important to them in both spheres.

The discourse of online learning has often in the past seen online, distance learning as a distinct *alternative* to an on-campus experience. This dichotomy does not exist in students' minds, rather they see a full-time on-campus experience as needing to be extremely rich in online learning and they are increasingly enthusiastic about flexibly combining a blended mixture of online interactions and working away from campus part-time, all to fit around their personal and work circumstances. Given the new student fees regime, this demand for greater flexibility in the mode of study through a degree programme is only likely to increase.

---

1 Collaborate to compete: seizing the opportunity of online learning for UK higher education: report to HEFCE by the Online Learning Task Force, January 2011. Available at http://www.hefce.ac.uk/learning/enhance/taskforce/

Another main message of the report challenges the assumption that all younger people, including students, are equally competent and comfortable with the use of pervasive technologies through mobile devices, the Web and so on. Again students recognised that in reality it is a much more nuanced picture. Many students are self-taught and admit to gaps in their skills. Those with technological fluency accept that their confidence in dealing with, evaluating and interacting with complex content and knowledge in an online environment is not necessarily well developed. There is, however, a strong desire from students for full engagement with learning development, as partners in this process with academics, rather than being regarded simply as passive recipients of learning.

As more and more course content is available online and embedded within institutional 'virtual learning environments', then the question arises as to what is the best use of face-to-face time and 'contact hours'. Both are highly valued by students but one might argue that there needs to be considerably more sophisticated debate about what is meant by these terms. Especially in a context that includes the growing availability of pod-casts and lectures online, of video presentations in parallel with lecture notes and PowerPoint presentations, and with all this content allowing time-shifting and knowledge acquisition at the pace and convenience of individual students. So, what is face-to-face time best for? And can virtual 'face-to-face' interactions be effective? Certainly there are many examples from the Open University and other leaders in distance learning, of excellent virtual face-to-face and group interactions – the synchronous technologies to support this have come on leaps and bounds in recent years, though it must be remembered that they are still in their infancy. Inspirational teaching and motivational engagement, with academics who are passionate about their subjects, are highly valued by students and ways of sustaining and developing this, whatever mode it is delivered in, is very much part of a student's assessment of what a quality education really means. The timeliness and depth of online assessment and feedback are also two critical elements contributing to perceived quality by students, something explored further by Sally Brown in her article.

In the Task Force we also examined the experiences of those in schools and colleges today and therefore what the likely expectations will soon be of higher education. We used information from Becta from 2009-10 which said that 93% of secondary schools had adopted a virtual learning environment (VLE) and 98% of colleges. Over 80% of secondary schools use VLEs for uploading and downloading homework, and for using and storing digital resources. Over 70% of schools see it as a 'high priority' to use online learning to extend learning beyond the classroom. I could go on… but if you combine this information with our knowledge of the rapidly increasing use of personal and mobile technologies, the internet, developments in super-fast broadband and mobile connections, and a range of social media tools, then the educational and technological imperative for universities become even clearer. Those sixteen year olds who were in school as the Becta 2009-10 cohort will be in universities next year, i.e. starting in 2012-13.

Unsurprisingly these driving forces led the Task Force to take a deeper look at how far universities are prepared for, and engaged strategically in, all that is demanded and expected by this and next generation students. Learning technology has long since been a preserve of the enthusiast, but the Task Force concluded that the whole institution needs to pay attention as a core part of strategy development and positioning, and as a holistic perspective when considering all that is meant by quality in teaching and learning. The Task Force report is rich and diverse in case studies of success in different types of institutions and in fulfilling different missions. They all repay further study and give a really good picture of what is already going on today. What they have in common is strong leadership as well as positive support and encouragement for academics and other colleagues – most successfully working in teams with a mix of intellectual leadership, pedagogic and content expertise, and technological enabling skills – to think about and engage with the new challenge.

Much of this agenda is not new, but arguably its time has come. The student demand is there, the technologies are widely available if not quite ubiquitous yet, and the student wish and need for flexibility in routes to higher level qualifications, from informal learning through to work-based learning, is ever more important. In the recent HEPI annual lecture[2] given by Jamil Salmi, The World Bank Tertiary Education Co-ordinator, argued that we all need to learn to learn and unlearn continuously, given the pace of new knowledge creation and redundancy, even within some three year degree programmes, and that undergraduates of today can anticipate five different jobs or professions in their careers. It is hard not to argue that online learning has a major role to play in this challenging but exciting future and we must be bold in embracing it.

Dame Lynne Brindley has been the Chief Executive of the British Library since 2000 and Chaired the 2009-11 HEFCE Online Learning Task Force.

The British Library is the national library of the United Kingdom and one of the world's greatest research libraries. Its collection exceeds 150 million separate items, including books, newspapers, manuscripts and sound recordings.

---

2   Flourish or Fail? Higher education in crisis – the global context. London, 23rd February 2011

Future trends in the information landscape

Alison Allden

The UK Higher Education (HE) sector relies on a complex network of information systems that underpin every aspect of academic and non-academic activity. These business information systems must support the whole learning life-cycle, including; course design, marketing, recruitment, enrolment, funding, achievement, credit transfer and alumni relations. Furthermore, there are systems that need to support the full range of research and enterprise processes within an institution. In addition to their operational role these systems produce data and information that is analysed and interpreted to inform institutions, funders and regulators, as well as a wider audience of students, parents and beyond. As the HE sector moves into new models of funding and regulation, the nature of this information, and the ways in which it will be used, are set to undergo radical change. Paramount is the focus on information, advice and guidance, for the student who is about to invest an increasing amount of money in their future through undertaking higher education.

Public information and the impact of policy

Historically, student data has driven the machinery of funding allocations by the funding council. The shift of funding in England from a central allocation model to a student purchase model will place greater emphasis than ever before on bottom-up data as the basis of information, advice and guidance for the applicant and increasingly as a marketing tool. While institutions have often quoted choice statistics in their marketing, the drive to the *student-as-investor* model will push demand for reliable predictions of return on investment. Graduate salary data has already been promoted in this way and the proposed sector-driven Key Information Set for prospective students will take some of these ideas further. Reliable data about the long-term career prospects of graduates (as well as meaningful comparison with non-graduates) is now being focused on to help future students decide which course is right for them – or indeed whether higher education is the best route or not. The expansion of the HE sector to include private providers of HE and a greater emphasis on local access through further education (FE) colleges makes the need for a comprehensive landscape of comparative information more important than ever.

The Coalition Government are also strong proponents of the Open Data agenda and increasingly HE institutions and sector agencies will face calls for more data to be made freely available. This is likely to mean not only greater volumes of data, but data at a more granular level. Enabling technologies are developing at a rapid pace and the desire to link, analyse and share data will be strong amongst the intelligent and technically savvy individuals that enter higher education. The availability of data and information has largely been managed by HE institutions in the past but the increasing demand for transparency is challenging the measured, rigorous and academic approach to the release of high quality, often peer reviewed and referenced, data. The risk of removing context and provenance from information is one that must be carefully managed if transparency is to play a meaningful part in providing public information.

The thirst for information and the wider availability of data will drive an expansion in the range of organisations and websites offering to interpret and advise on higher education choices. Over the years the sector has had a sometimes uncomfortable relationship with newspaper league tables, and many have argued that modern universities are too complex and dynamic to be represented through simple ranking systems that are often based largely on analyses of full-time undergraduate students. However, the sector cannot ignore the impact that these publications have on individual student choices and the broader perception of what is a good university. The *student-as-investor* model will drive a rapid expansion in both the number and scope of league tables, as well as other forms of comparative analysis products. Although a university degree is a far less generic offering than, say, car insurance, the success of price and feature comparison web sites in the financial services industry might well be replicated in higher education some day. In this context the provider-derived, comparable and kite-marked Key Information Set (KIS) for courses is likely to replace an authoritative and trusted information resource.

The drive for efficiencies and improvements in service will push the need for ever greater levels of interoperability between data systems across the sector. Changes in student funding might drive the expansion of flexible or modular programmes and further press the need for credit accumulation and transfer schemes. Increasingly, students of the future might look for alternatives to the traditional model of full-time, continuous higher education as they seek to spread their studies over time and across multiple locations.

Regulating the sector

Data and information requests are a key element of regulation mechanisms across the sector. Research undertaken for the Higher Education Better Regulation Group (HEBRG) has unveiled a broad range of information reporting channels for various professional, statutory and regulatory bodies (PSRBs). In addition to the reporting that accompanies core funding council grants, significant amounts of data are provided to support other streams of funding (e.g. NHS activity and research funding) and professional and regulatory bodies that accredit specific courses. Depending on the nature and variety of their provision, an individual institution can face a complex web of different reporting channels for detailed student data, making the issues of 'burden' and consistency in reporting a significant challenge for providers. As regulation mechanisms evolve, the associated burdens will face ever greater scrutiny and the sector should work with PSRBs to achieve standard mechanisms and definitions for reporting. It is likely that the public investment through the loan system, the desire to support social mobility and the evidence for outcomes and impact, will together require an information-dependent regulatory framework, yet to be determined in the delayed HE White Paper.

Institutions as information customers

Increasingly, higher education institutions are utilising sector-level data to analyse and benchmark their performance. Institutions have become more demanding customers of information in recent years and increasingly utilise tools such as HESA's Higher Education Information Database for Institutions (HEIDI) and commercially available benchmarking services. The challenge of making valid comparisons between complex and autonomous organisations like universities depends on access to data from a variety of sources that are both trustworthy and comparable at a fine level of granularity. It might be assumed increased competition between providers and a desire to understand areas of competitive advantage will drive demands for robust, detailed and comparable information from across the sector. At the same time there are concerns that the accepted benefits of sharing and making data available across the sector, which has been prevalent, may be threatened by heightened competition and the need to retain a competitive edge.

Technology

As discussed, the HE sector operates a network of data systems that manage the entire student lifecycle from admissions to alumni relations, as well as research and enterprise activity. The technology that supports these systems continues to develop at a rapid pace and the ability to process and share large volumes of complex data between systems has improved dramatically in recent years. Increasingly the focus of system development is on interoperability and the desire to grow the value of data by re-using it across different applications. This not only saves costs but also ensures higher quality and consistency to support decision making, the research infrastructure and of increasing importance, the student experience.

Easing the burden and unlocking the potential – data standards and the future vision

In spite of the numerous drivers for change, the HE information landscape is currently a disparate collection of systems, data definitions and lexicons. Even fundamental building blocks, such as the concept of a "Course", create difficulties both within institutions and across the sector. Students flow through higher education acquiring a plethora of personal identifiers as they go and the interfaces between different data systems are often compromised due to differences in the underlying data structures and definitions. The information that flows from the sector – from the combination of these different systems - is subsequently of lower quality and higher cost than it otherwise could be One goal to be achieved is not only to manage the flow and exchange of information within the sector but to link data from schools and onto employment, to support the learning transition and achievement of individual learners. Likewise the investment in research, its impact and the contribution that higher education make to the economy, needs to be tracked and evidenced. There is a mechanism that will help to achieve this and that is through the adoption of open and agreed standards. The importance of standards has become more evident in recent years, and the adoption of agreed technical and information standards should become an imperative rather than remain optional.

To realise the potential of the future HE information landscape we need to promote better ways to link and share data between different educational providers and agencies; the technology will enable it and the stakeholders will demand it. But this can only be achieved through the adoption of standards, and the rationalisation of identifiers. There are two ways of thinking about data standards: the top-down model has a central authority developing, consulting on and publishing standards, or at least specifications that they offer for adoption; the bottom-up model sees standards evolve as the sector identifies standard data solutions to common information problems. Whichever way they develop, the adoption of open technical standards, standard data models, definitions and identifiers will reduce costs, increase quality and enhance the linking and comparability of information across the education system. HESA is promoting this vision of a better connected information landscape. It is a vision that the sector must invest in to support the progression of students into higher education and record the benefits to them of that engagement. Good information will ensure that higher education is properly understood and appreciated as a public good that hugely benefits the UK, and that it is regarded as a social and economic priority accordingly.

Alison Allden is the Chief Executive of HESA, is a Fellow of the British Computer Society, sits on the JISC (Joint Information Systems Committee) Board and is also a member of the Information Standards Board.

__HESA (the Higher Education Statistics Agency)__ is the official agency for the collection, analysis and dissemination of comprehensive information about higher education in the UK.

How Open Data, data literacy and Linked Data will revolutionise higher education

Derek McAuley, Hanif Rahemtulla, James Goulding and Catherine Souch

"Open Data" refers to the philosophical and methodological approach to democratising data, enabling individuals, communities and organisations to access and create value through the reuse of non-sensitive, publicly available information. This data is typically available online at no cost to citizen groups, non-governmental-organisations (NGOs) and businesses. Some view this as the logical conclusion to Freedom of Information (FoI) Acts in various countries – if citizens can ask for the data, why not simply publish it in the first place?

Today, Open Data is gathering momentum, and forms part of a global movement, linked to other movements such as Open Access and Open Source. The Open Data Initiatives will, it is envisaged, support greater transparency and accountability within Government, as well as leading to economic development in commercial sectors and improved public sector service delivery. Integral to this vision is that information hitherto held in hidden databases is opened to the public and, furthermore, released in a form that facilitates easy reuse.

To date, the Open Data movement has created great excitement in developer communities. Social and commercial entrepreneurs are producing a seemingly endless stream of innovative applications that repurpose and enrich publicly available data, across multiple sectors, including; health, transport, education and the environment. This new wave of creativity is characterised by Sir Tim Berners-Lee (creator of the World Wide Web) as the combination of information, creative vision and digital technology.

However, smart governments should not rely solely on the organic growth produced by entrepreneurs. Rather, as argued by Eaves;

> "forward-looking governments – those that want an engaged citizenry, a 21st-century workforce and a creative, knowledge-based economy in their jurisdiction – will reach out to universities, colleges and schools and encourage them to get their students using, visualising, writing about and generally engaging with Open Data[1]."

---

1   Eaves (2010) Learning from Libraries: The Literacy Challenge of Open Data. Available at: www.eaves.ca [Accessed June 2010]

This will foster a sense of opportunity among this generation, to interact and participate in this wave of innovation and change, empowering citizens to improve services, reduce costs and boost productivity.

To illustrate, consider www.police.uk which had recently launched at the time of writing, amid a fanfare of publicity. It was immediately pilloried from various quarters for overloaded servers, sluggish service (indicating, at least, an intrigued public) and inaccurate data. If the latter is true, then surely this was a great opportunity to encourage the bottom-up correction of a large public database that police agencies work with on a daily basis. However, few voices pointed to such opportunities, or highlighted how combining this data with other information, for example economic data from ONS, could help geography, sociology and criminology researchers develop valuable insights into the relationship between employment and crime.

Such researchers within higher education establishments are at the vanguard of the Open Data movement, whether as evangelists, users or technologists. Higher education has pioneered the use of web technologies, with institutions making large amounts of information available to students, commercial partners, funding agencies and staff. Yet there is still much that can only be accessed through FoI requests, and most data resides on static web pages, rather than in common data formats that enable data reuse. In the UK, the Joint Information Systems Committee (JISC) has been developing such open data standards, with initiatives such as ePortfolios and course definitions, which if adopted by a sufficiently large proportion of the sector would enable a wave of innovation.

Integral to this growth in innovative data uses and repurposing is training in *Data Literacy* within higher education. Data literacy – defined here as the ability to identify, retrieve, evaluate and use information to both ask and answer meaningful questions – is an important civic skill that forms the foundation of an innovative knowledge economy and increasingly data-driven society. To demonstrate, one needs only to reflect on a recent statement by Richard Sterling (Former Head of *data.gov.uk*). In July 2010 he acknowledged that the public are already struggling to make sense of the huge volume of datasets published online, expressing concerns that individuals may be coming to conclusions that "weren't quite valid" after browsing the 5,850 data sets available on *data.gov.uk*. Sterling attributes this to the format of the information (e.g. structure, configuration and pre-processing) impacting deleteriously on the capacity of end users to make use of the data. As Davis[2] states, much public sector

---

2 Davis, T., (2010) Open Data, Democracy and Public Sector Reform. Available at: http://www. practicalparticipation.co.uk/ [Accessed July 2010]

information is "simply not collected in a usable form at present"[3] and the systematic organisation of information is not a neutral act, involving decisions that impact both on its interpretation and future use[4]. For example, with regard to the recent crime statistics data, the conclusions that can be drawn are very clearly a function of both how data is collected and the degree of aggregation granularity used to preserve privacy of individual households.

Further, addressing these challenges by providing online query and visualisation tools to "make it easier to analyse and visualise the data" as proposed by Sterling, assumes that the public have sufficient knowledge and skills to interpret and use data, and know the sources of uncertainties generated in the conflation of different open datasets[5]. Even something as simple as *where something happens* is a complex problem; for example data recorded based on local government boundaries, which are subject to change, can only be interpreted rationally with access to a historical archive of such boundaries.

Herein lies an important distinction between the often-conflated memes ('meme' is a relatively newly coined term, attributed to Richard Dawkins, which describes a unit of social information, ideas or beliefs that is transmitted from one person or group to another, analogous to genes) of *Open Data* and *Linked Data*. While the former represents an unequivocal step forward in increased access to, and public ownership of large data sets, it is the latter that holds the potential to be a powerful, positive and disruptive force in higher education. Meltzoff *et al.* reported that;

> "insights from many different fields are converging to create a new science of learning that may transform education practice. [6]"

It is Linked Data, with its facility to cross-correlate traditionally disparate, ring-fenced research resources, such as scientific, geographical, economic and sociological datasets, that will be a central tool in this transformation.

Linked Data, which uses familiar web-based URL addresses to provide links between Open Data sources, allows higher education to benefit from a 'network effect'

3   Allan, R., (2009). The Power of Government Information. In J. Gøtze & C. B. Pedersen, eds. State of the eUnion: Government 2.0 and Onwards. Author House. p.01

4   Snowdon (2010), p.01 Its information to data we need, not DIKW. Cognitive Edge. Available at: www.cognitive-edge.com/blogs/dave/2010/05/its_information_to_data_we_nee.php [Accessed May 2010].

5   Sterling (2010, p.01) Open data hard to understand, says data.gov.uk chief. Available at: www.information-age.com [Accessed June 2010].

6   Meltzoff, A. N., Kuhl, P. K., Movellan, J., and Sejnowski, T. J. (2009). *Foundations for a new science of learning*. Science 325, 284–288.

as educational data is liberated from its traditional silos. Richer interconnected information environments will produce richer learning environments and a host of new opportunities: simplifying resource discovery and promoting personal exploration of material; supporting integration of distributed discourse while encouraging referencing skills; enhancing construction of both personal and group knowledge while promoting self-actuated learning; facilitating better argumentation and critical thinking skills through advanced reasoning over large volumes of resources; and because Linked Data represents a powerful tool for independent learning, it does all this with the added benefit of further disintermediating educators.

Realisation of this potential has not only begun, but continues apace. Hard sciences have paved the way through projects such as *Bio2RDF* and *Linked Life Data* which provide immense corpora of life-science information. Economists are harnessing Linked Data from public sector bodies such as the *World Bank* and the *Office of National Statistics,* as well as from a growing number of private sector producers (such as *Xignite* who provide access to live financial information). Geographers enjoy the facilities offered by geospatial Linked Data services such as *GeoNames* and *LinkedGeoData*, with its 350 million queryable geographical features, and Sociologists now have unprecedented access to the European Union's statistical data, thanks to the *Reise* project, with its 3 billion queryable *Eurostat* derived facts.

The value of these resources to higher education lies not merely in openness and accessibility, but in their interconnectivity. The capability to query as well as browse, to benefit from *data fusion* mechanisms, generates both novel research discoveries and compelling educational experiences. Consider, for instance, the educational worth, research value and policy implications of being able to tie socio-economic data from *Reise*, with epidemiological patterns referenced by *Linked Life Data,* then joining this with the travel patterns indicated within *LinkedGeoData.*

Linked Data shows signs of achieving traction in higher education. However,

> *"despite undoubted progress, the green shoots of a Linked Data ecology remain delicate[7]"*

and, as such, we must take great care to reinforce the progress of this revolution. Higher education technologies require scalable inter-disciplinary design, and although Linked Data affords us exactly that, policies surrounding it must be grounded in communication and sharing of expertise amongst research disciplines. A number of cross-cutting issues stand out, but of these *Information Literacy* is the most pressing.

---

7   Miller, P., (2010) Commissioned Report: "Linked Data Horizon Scan", Joint Information Systems Committee (JISC), 2010.

With the *DBPedia* project now exposing *Wikipedia* as linked data, and services such as *freebase* expanding rapidly, educating students to distinguish between good and bad resources is paramount. For our part we must not only provide methodologies for making this distinction, but actively ensure that such distinctions are achievable in the first place. Bechhofer argues that we must therefore bring our attention to bear on publishing requirements such as data *provenance*, *quality* and *attribution* – and that without addressing these considerations, simply publishing data into the cloud will not sufficiently meet the requirements of reuse[8].

The Open Data revolution and emerging technologies such as Linked Data offer exciting opportunities for higher education, allowing substantial learning challenges to be met by interlinking resources across disciplines and institutions. However, policy must attempt to reinforce progress already made, encouraging institutions to openly release their data in a linkable form, to deploy applications that use these resources within their educational programs and, importantly, to enhance emerging data vocabularies rather than engaging in top-down didactic creation of new ones. However, many challenges remain. There are fundamental epistemological differences in how different cultures, communities and disciplines (and even academics within a single discipline), view the same information and hence we need to be aware of and embrace different, even conflicting, vocabularies. New applications of data will revolutionise higher education, but it must take the lead in driving up data literacy amongst staff, students and the wider population.

Professor Derek McAuley *is Professor of Digital Economy in the School of Computer Science and Director of Horizon, a Digital Economy Research Institute, at the University of Nottingham, and Affiliated Lecturer at the University of Cambridge Computer Laboratory. He is a Fellow of the British Computer Society and member of the UKCRC, a computing research expert panel of the IET and BCS.*

Dr. Hanif Rahemtulla *is Geospatial Scientist at the University of Nottingham and External Lecturer and Honorary Fellow at University College London. His research is principally focused in the areas of geographic information policy focusing on Open and Linked Data, the handling and analysis of environmental information, and wider philosophical issues on the societal impacts of Information Communication Technologies.*

Dr. James Goulding *is an early career researcher with a rapidly growing list of international publications across the fields of data theory, location based services, information retrieval and ubiquitous computing. Extremely experienced software engineer with a passion for Open and Linked data and an extensive range of programming skills, specialising in mobile technologies, distributed databases and artificial intelligence techniques.*

---

8   Bechhofer et al. (2010) "Why Linked Data is Not Enough for Scientists". 6th IEEE e-Science conference 2010.

Horizon Digital Economy Research at the University of Nottingham represents an initial £40million investment by Research Councils UK, The University of Nottingham and more than 100 academic and industrial partners in both a Research Hub and Doctoral Training Centre within the RCUK Digital Economy programme. Horizon brings together researchers with backgrounds in computer science, the geospatial sciences, engineering, psychology, sociology, business, social science, law and the arts to build-in an understanding of people and society in technology developments from the outset, and to ensure users benefit from these advances.

Dr. Catherine Souch is Head of Research and Higher Education at the Royal Geographical Society (with the Institute of British Geographers). Previously, she was Professor of Geography at Indiana University, USA.

The Royal Geographical Society (with Institute of British Geographers) was founded in 1830 and is a world centre for geography: supporting research, education, expeditions and fieldwork, and promoting public engagement and informed enjoyment of the world.

Section five – How can students be best served?

Mature policies for higher education access

Nick Pearce

Over the last two decades, higher education has been a growth sector in almost all advanced and developing economies. On average across Organisation for Economic Co-operation and Development (OECD) countries, graduation rates from university-level education have increased by a huge 21 percentage points in the past 13 years. The rate of change has been such that the UK – despite large increases in higher education enrolments – has slipped to mid-table in the OECD graduation rankings.

OECD graduation rankings 1995-2008[1]

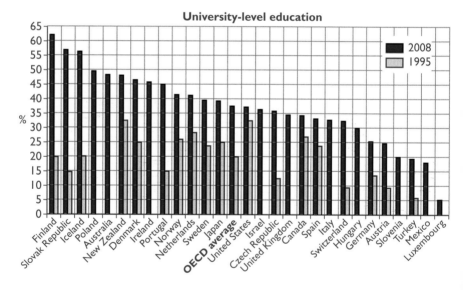

However, expansion in UK higher education has been accompanied by a significant widening of access. The gains have not simply accrued to the middle classes. Research by the Higher Education Funding Council for England (HEFCE)[2] shows that the likelihood of those from the lowest participation areas entering higher education has increased by 30 per cent over the last five years and by 50 per cent over the last 15 years. The

---

1 OECD (2010), Education at a Glance 2010, Table A3.2
2 HEFCE (2010) *Trends in young participation in higher education*

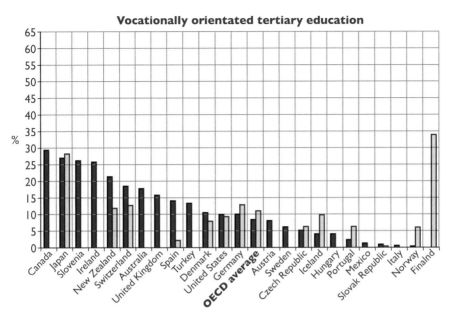

Vocationally orientated tertiary education

gap between the participation rates of young people from the most advantaged and the most disadvantaged areas has been narrowing, both in proportional terms and percentage point terms, since the mid 2000s.

This success in widening access is largely attributable to the long-term effects of school reforms, dating back to the introduction of the GCSE in the 1980s, which first spurred expansion in staying-on rates. More recently, rising school standards and progress in the closing of social class gaps in 16-19 educational participation, aided by Educational Maintenance Allowances (EMAs), has provided a platform for increased higher education applications from young people from low income households. In turn, this increase in demand has been met by an increased supply of places, facilitated by the funding secured from the introduction of tuition fees. In this way, policymakers have broadly achieved their goals of expanding enrolments, widening access and maintaining standards of higher education. Fees did not deter wider access so much as provide the funding to enable it to happen. Critically, however, access widened because there were more places on offer: this will not be the case in the years ahead.

In contrast to this story, fairer access to the most selective institutions has not improved – indeed, on some measures, it has got worse. The most advantaged 20 per cent of young people were around six times more likely to attend selective universities in the mid-1990s than the most disadvantaged 40 per cent. This had increased to around seven times more likely by the mid-2000s. Moreover, as the Sutton Trust has documented, independent (private) school pupils are over 22 times more likely to enter a highly selective university than those disadvantaged state school children who are entitled to Free School Meals (FSM).

The reasons for such disparities are to be found largely in prior attainment, although it is noticeable that leading universities, such as King's College London and University College London, recruit significantly higher proportions of students from low income backgrounds than other Russell Group members (which may be attributed, inter alia, to their geographical proximity to those students, use of contextual admissions policies and outreach programmes).

One lesser remarked aspect of this lack of progress is how inequality in attainment in science A-levels drives access to selective universities. It is almost impossible to apply to Russell Group universities in courses such as medicine, engineering and the natural sciences without A or A* grades in science subjects at A-level. The odds of achieving grades A or B at A-level are 2-3 times higher for those who take separate sciences than for those entered for 'core' (dual or triple combined subjects, sometimes with 'additional' science subjects) science at GCSE. And yet until recently, there has been a virtual apartheid in the schools system between, on the one hand, independent and grammar schools offering single science GCSEs, and on the other the comprehensive schools that only offer the combined 'core' qualifications.

The dominance of the independent and grammar schools in higher grade science A-levels is clearly visible in the 2010 entries for Physics.

A-level Physics grades A/B[3]

Fortunately, a remarkable catch-up process has taken place in the maintained comprehensive sector in recent years.

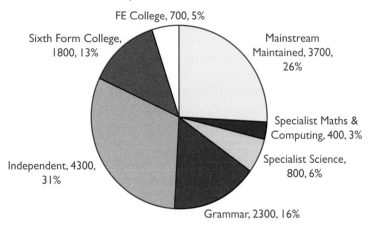

FE College, 700, 5%
Sixth Form College, 1800, 13%
Mainstream Maintained, 3700, 26%
Specialist Maths & Computing, 400, 3%
Specialist Science, 800, 6%
Independent, 4300, 31%
Grammar, 2300, 16%

---

3   Department for Education (2011), *Maths & Science Education: the Supply of High Achievers at A-level*, DfE Research Report DFE-RR079

Increase in schools offering GCSE Triple Science, 2008-2010[4]

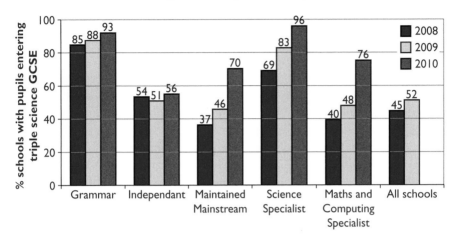

These improvements should underpin stronger A-level performance in the sciences in comprehensive schools, sixth form and further education (FE) colleges in the future, broadening the base of applicants in these subjects to selective universities.

Of course, it is too soon to tell whether tuition fees of £6,000 or £9,000 will deter applicants to higher education from low income homes. If tuition fees were a deterrent in themselves, recent progress in widening access would not have taken place. But demand for higher education is not infinitely elastic, and the experience of the USA shows that it is more likely to be students from low to middle income households who lose out, rather than the rich or poor: another case of the 'squeezed middle'. It is young people from these backgrounds who will feel the loss of the Educational Maintenance Allowance – the first rung on the ladder to higher education after GCSEs – most keenly.

Mature access

Yet putting these contemporary debates in wider context, it should be recalled that the greatest steps forward in broadening access to higher education have come when the needs of mature students, seeking part-time local or distance learning, have taken precedence in policy. Tony Crosland created the polytechnic sector precisely to expand opportunities for adults who wanted courses to fit in with their working and family lives. The Open University was founded on similar principles. These institutions eschewed the Oxbridge and plate glass residential model of the university that the Robbins Report had endorsed, preferring to democratise access to higher education by creating new institutional structures and methods for learning. In large part, they were successful in this endeavour. Today mature students account for the majority of first year undergraduate students (382,195 in English higher education institutions in 2009-10, compared to 333,225 under 21 years.)

Unfortunately, subsequent changes to government support for students, dominated by the residential model of higher education for young people, lagged behind the institutional creativity of the 1960s and 1970s. Historically, part-time students, as well as those in further education, have fared much worse in the allocation of public funding for student support, only securing additional entitlements after Labour came to power in 1997, and even then remaining excluded from the main student loan and grant system. One of the least noticed (in public debate at least) but most welcome elements of the current UK Coalition Government's reform package is that part-time students studying at 33% of a full-time course will be entitled to tuition fee loans.

In the future, renewed impetus for achieving greater equality in access to higher education must come from expanding places. This will now have to wait until the next Comprehensive Spending Review in 2014, when the focus should be on shorter, initial higher education programmes (such as Foundation Degrees), work-based and part-time learning, and the creation of new routes into higher education for higher-level apprentices. All of these have lower unit costs than traditional full-time higher education and are areas of provision that would most benefit from further expansion. Further education colleges also want to provide more places 'off quota' at no extra cost to the government and they should be allowed to do so. Whilst school reform can help level the playing field in access to university for young people, social justice in higher education will not be achieved without putting mature students at the forefront of policy.

Nick Pearce is Director of IPPR, the Institute for Public Policy Research.

IPPR is the UK's leading progressive think tank. We produce rigorous research and innovative policy ideas for a fair, democratic and sustainable world. We are open and independent in how we work, and with offices in London and the North of England, IPPR spans a full range of local and national policy debates. Our international partnerships extend IPPR's influence and reputation across the world.

Securing the future of postgraduate education

Geoff Whitty

The UK Government was slow to recognise a threat to the future health of postgraduate provision in English universities. Initially, it seemed to accept the 2010 Browne report's assumption that, not only was there no need to extend the proposed undergraduate student support package to postgraduates, existing state funding to institutions for most taught Master's courses could cease on the same basis as for undergraduate courses.[1] Ministers claimed that withdrawal of funding for courses would be offset by an increase in public funding for student support. Yet no new support package for postgraduate students has so far been proposed.

What is at stake?

At first, leaders of postgraduate institutions for the arts and social sciences led efforts to highlight the dangers. Subsequently, there has been a wider recognition that any threat to the funding of postgraduate education could have a serious impact on universities and the future strength of UK research. British Academy president, Sir Adam Roberts, asked:

> *"if fees reform puts graduates off postgraduate study, where will academia find its new blood?"*[2]

But it is not just an issue for the future of arts subjects in UK universities, important as that is. In a report for the previous government, Adrian Smith argued that the skills of postgraduates were:

> *"critical for tackling major business challenges and driving innovation and growth."*[3]

Indeed, the wider consequences of not getting postgraduate education right could be considerable for the health of the professions and for the UK's competitiveness in the global economy.

The Government itself has noticed that school teachers in high-performing countries are educated to Master's level. Yet, while encouraging more teachers to take such courses, it has stopped funding a scheme that enabled them to do so.[4] And, in a report last year, the inventor Sir James Dyson claimed that, in 2008, only 70 out of

---

1   Browne Report, *Securing a Sustainable Future for Higher Education in the UK*, October 2010.

2   Adam Roberts, 'It's hard to go on', *Times Higher Education*, 23rd December 2010.

3   Adrian Smith, *One Step Beyond: Making the most of postgraduate education*, Department of Business, Innovation and Skills, March 2010.

4   James Noble-Rogers, 'Why teachers need to carry on learning', *Independent*, 24th March 2011.

3,825 additional postgraduate engineering students were from the UK. He recently warned that this could have a huge impact on the economy and called for more government grants to enable UK students to study at postgraduate level.[5]

Browne took comfort from the fact that, under previous arrangements, overall enrolments at postgraduate level increased by 25% between 2002-03 and 2008-09 and by 46% for taught Master's courses. Yet rates for home students were significantly lower, even if they do seem to have increased somewhat in the last two years. As some of those students were already repaying undergraduate loans, this might suggest there is no problem. However, increased debt and the removal of state funding for most courses will now take us into uncharted territory.

New access issues

It is not just the number of students that matters, but also the composition of the student body. Browne quoted figures that showed private school students already more likely than their state school peers to undertake postgraduate study.[6]

The backgrounds of postgraduates and undergraduates[7]

	Privately Educated	State school educated
Postgraduate population	17%	83%
Undergraduate population	14%	86%
Total population	7%	93%

In arguing for *"fairer financial support for postgraduate students"* in 2009, Alan Milburn suggested that a lack of postgraduate funding for access to the professions had serious implications for social mobility.[8] Evidence from other countries is that, as undergraduate qualifications become the norm, postgraduate study is an increasingly important social sorting mechanism.

Even after the Government's reforms, fees for home undergraduate students will remain regulated. At Master's level, they are not. Average fees for a one-year course for a home student rose to £4,000 last year, while an MBA cost an average of £12,000.[9] Fees will rise significantly when the subsidy is removed and, when undergraduate

---

5   Hannah Richardson, 'Lack of top researchers could harm UK plc, warns Dyson', BBC News website, 15th February, 2011.

6   Browne, *op cit*

7   Browne Report drawn from Sutton Trust, itself drawing on DLHE data

8   Milburn Report, *Unleashing Aspiration: the Final Report of the Panel on Fair Access to the Professions*, July 2009.

9   Lucy Tobin, 'Will a master's get you a job?', *Guardian*, 15th February 2011.

fees triple from 2012, universities are unlikely to price postgraduate courses below undergraduate ones.

Compared with provision for undergraduates, support for postgraduates is 'hit or miss'. Research Council studentships are available for some students, while some others have access to career development loans. Some get support from their employers, but many fund themselves, particularly if they study part-time. Cost sharing is already widespread at postgraduate level, but the proposed removal of any state subsidy would make the extent of a student's own means to contribute increasingly important.

Terence Kealey has claimed that:

> "the UK market in taught postgraduate courses has long been liberalised, so its fees are correspondingly high, yet demand rises inexorably."[10]

He, like Browne, may have been unduly influenced by a Business School model. While higher degrees as a whole do bring benefits to individuals and the Exchequer, not all subjects command high fees nor do they all produce impressive returns. Smith's report showed that recent postgraduates earned on average £23,500 six months after graduating – a postgraduate premium of around 24%.[11] However, Business and Administrative Studies postgraduates earned 36% more than first-degree holders, while Languages and Engineering students gained only an 11% premium.[12]

In some arts subjects, individual financial benefits from study at this level could be minimal, despite its wider social benefits. Future funding options need to take this into account. Furthermore, the majority of home postgraduate students are part-time and, unless things change, they will face the triple disincentive of increased undergraduate debt, higher postgraduate fees and no student support package.

Ways forward

Browne himself accepted a need to monitor the impact of higher undergraduate fees and David Willetts has acknowledged that:

> "it would be clearly detrimental to this country if we saw a big fall in postgraduate numbers".

10   Terence Kealey 'Free the market: take the cap off tuition fees', *The Times*, 29th March 2011.

11   Smith, *op cit*

12   See also Nigel O'Leary and Peter Sloane, 'The Return to a University Education in Great Britain', *National Institute Economic Review* 193:75 2005.

He has now asked Sir Adrian Smith to review the future of postgraduate study in the new funding environment.[13]

So what options are open to the Government? Southampton Vice-Chancellor, Don Nutbeam, uses his Australian experience to champion a single loan system for undergraduate and postgraduate education, with a lifetime cap on the amount that can be borrowed. This would provide flexibility in relation to individual students' lifetime learning needs and changing economic conditions, while maintaining financial control by government. He warns that:

"the alternative is a system in which UK universities continue to operate in a global market place...from which our own students become increasingly excluded."[14]

If Nutbeam's proposals are not feasible in the short term, some measures will need to be put in place before students emerge with increased undergraduate debt. Among those floated have been maintenance of teaching funding for postgraduate courses and an endowment fund to support 'need-blind' entry for home students in some subjects. Others might include repayment 'holidays' for those returning to study part-time while repaying their undergraduate debts, or a more comprehensive and comprehensible system of career development loans. Employers will need to make a greater contribution, perhaps incentivised by tax breaks. For key professions like health, social work, education and defence the state could act as a surrogate employer and provide other incentives. A 'one stop shop' for information on courses and funding for postgraduates would also help.

There is, of course, a need for continuing debate about the meaning of graduate skills and the nature of postgraduate education, as well as about the balance to be struck between undergraduate and postgraduate provision. However, such debates should take place in a context where access to postgraduate education is a realistic possibility for those who can benefit from it. It would be ironic if the new undergraduate arrangements proved to be more equitable than their critics fear, only to find that inequities are reintroduced via that part of the system that has so far been neglected in the funding debate.

Professor Geoff Whitty *is Director Emeritus at the Institute of Education, University of London.*

13 David Willetts, speech to meeting of Universities UK, London, 25th February 2011.

14 Don Nutbeam, 'Postgraduates need financial support', Guardian, 1st February 2011. See also 'Encourage lifetime learning with a flexible, integrated loan system', Times Higher Education, 1st July 2010.

Meeting the challenge of heightened expectations: how universities can enhance the student experience

Paul Marshall

The passage of new tuition fee legislation in December 2010 will be marked for future generations as a turning point in the history of the UK HE sector. The merits of the withdrawal of the state from the blanket subsidy of undergraduate degree programs and the transfer of the costs to the student has been much discussed, debated, argued and indeed, rioted upon. These debates, however, have created a foggy cloud under which the wider debate over the fundamentally important long term vision for the delivery of the highest quality student experience, has somewhat been lost.

In its submission to the Browne Review, the 1994 Group argued that the primary concern was to maintain quality so that universities were able to: strengthen the economy, deliver novel solutions to major challenges through research, and develop a world-class highly skilled workforce. HEFCE's Financial Sustainability Strategy Group, which reported in early 2009, concluded that the sector was already papering over the cracks in the delivery of the student experience. Its conclusion was that total student funding needed to increase by around 20%[1] to reverse the decline of provision. I share with the 1994 Group and HEFCE this fundamental belief, that universities need long-term sustainable funding to maintain the quality of the academic experience, meet students' rising expectations and develop the highly skilled, well-rounded graduates that our nation needs. In the future, this quality can only be maintained by increasing funding. This means achieving and maintaining additionality on the current income level per student. I therefore support, as the only viable option, the government's reforms to the graduate contribution system. However if we are to meet the requirements of taxpayers, students and employers, then simple additionality of funding is not enough. All universities must make a commitment to demonstrably enhance the student experience.

We need to think about what this means. 'Student Experience' is a wide-ranging term meaning different things to different kinds of students. An 18-year-old undergraduate or foundation degree student, living away from parents for the first time and discovering independence, has a very different experience of university to a 40-year-old masters student, living at home with partner and children, balancing a full-time job with part-time study. Both encounter a vastly different experience to that of a student

---

1   Financial Sustainability Strategy Group, The sustainability of learning and teaching in English higher education, Feb 2006 Access via http://www.hefce.ac.uk/finance/fundinghe/trac/fssg/FSSGreport.pdf

from China, who is getting to know a new language and culture as well as new learning material. There is no such thing as a standard student, and in the future successful universities will be those that don't just offer a standard student experience. They must be responsive, making sure that every student encounters university life on the terms that best meet their own particular expectations.

There are three levels to this type of responsive student experience.

First, at application. The learning experience begins well before university for each prospective student. It's up to all universities to recognise this and make sure that the process of choosing, and applying for courses is backed up with solid information, advice, and guidance. Transparency over contact time, assessment criteria and teaching staff will contribute to realistic academic expectations, but a range of other information also needs to be made available to prospective students.

Enhanced information on graduate employment and earnings potential will encourage course choices that complement future career aspirations. The Destination of Leavers from HE survey is useful, but taken at just six months following graduation it does not form an accurate reflection of the overall impact of university on graduates. It also overlooks students choosing to go on to further study rather than entering the employment marketplace. Other measures must be developed to enhance information in this area. For example, the longitudinal version of this survey, as it is taken 3½ years after graduation, provides a more realistic picture of the careers graduates will have chosen. There is a need for this survey to be developed, enhanced and made more robust in the future, to avoid an over-reliance on the 6 month survey.

Beyond this, the application level of the student experience should provide a genuine insight into what life at university will be like. The National Student Survey is fundamental to understanding the undergraduate student experience and must continue. Building on existing practice where possible, surveys capturing the experiences of post-graduates should also be established or enhanced in the future.

The second level of the student experience is university life itself. Students paying higher fees will have increased expectations of facilities and academic quality, which universities should all work to meet. There is a clear link between levels and quality of support, facilities and resources on offer to students, and how satisfied they are with their experience at university. Potentially working alongside the private sector, improvements to a university's physical infrastructure are a key area in which to enhance the student experience. Long-term efforts should continue to be made across the sector to make physical infrastructure more student friendly.

There's also an opportunity to add extra value. Universities should be partnerships between staff and students, with the student voice promoted and listened to. It is important for universities to make clear statements on the reciprocal relationships between students and universities in the development of knowledge and skills. A mature relationship is required with the NUS and local students' unions to build mutual trust alongside sometimes challenging debates.

The final level of the student experience is graduate. Universities should make every effort to ensure graduates can flourish throughout their lives and careers. The graduate employment market is extremely competitive and it is crucial that students are well equipped during their time at university to progress and achieve their potential in the workplace. All graduates should leave university as mature, well-rounded individuals with clearly recognisable skills which will help them in employment.

One way of achieving this is through co-curricular activity and awards, run in parallel to degree programmes. These not only enhance the overall experience for students, but are routes through which to meet employers' demand for skills obtained outside the academic curriculum.

Resourcing is clearly a key challenge to delivering this activity, especially to larger numbers of students. The Government should support for co-curricular activity by creating incentives for employers, such as schemes in which the government matches employers' contributions – whether these are cash or in kind.

Finally, graduates should experience the very highest academic standards. High quality, engaging teaching, complemented by world class research, creates a culture of excellence which will serve graduates, their employers and ultimately the entire economy well, long into the future.

In his 2010 speech at the Conservative Party Conference, David Willetts, Minister for Universities and Science made a clear commitment to future students.

> *"We cannot expect people to pay more after they graduate if they have not been properly taught ... I want to be able to look students in the eye and say they are getting a better education in return for the higher contribution they will make."*

Although it is a time of enormous change in higher education, none of us should be fearful. We should take up the opportunity to enhance the already excellent promise of UK universities. Rising to the challenge of raised student expectations provides powerful motivation for institutions to enhance the student experience, empowering applicants, students, and graduates to ensure they reap the benefits of their investment.

We must directly respond to the challenge laid down by government. It is wrong to expect taxpayers and the students to invest without clear evidence of return. It is up to universities to make those returns clearer in the future.

Paul Marshall is Executive Director of The 1994 Group. He is responsible for the management of all Group activity including policy development, government liaison and stakeholder relations. He is also a member of the UCAS Qualification Information Review Reference Group, CMI Academy Employer Board and the Research Concordat Executive Group.

The 1994 Group brings together 19 world class universities and is one of the UK's most influential voices on higher education policy. The Group works to promote excellence in research and teaching so that students can enjoy an outstanding learning experience and universities can contribute to social and economic wellbeing.

The best way to predict the future is to invent it: ensuring the STEM higher education pipeline

Paul Jackson

The UK has a proud tradition in engineering and manufacturing and if we are to ensure a bright future, we need more engineers. With a decline in the number of 18 year olds[1] over the next decade and a demand for 587,000 new workers in the manufacturing sector over a similar period[2], it has never been more important to encourage young people to like science, choose to study science and, ultimately, to choose a career in engineering. Two key questions impact the scale of economic benefit achievable: are schools and other routes producing the right foundations for higher education and do higher education institutions (HEIs) deliver the best degrees for the real world of engineers?

Recognising that engineering degrees in the UK use an accreditation process that involves the professional bodies, with clear links to industry, the focus here is on the first question.

Young people's experience of science, technology, engineering and mathematics (STEM) at school, and the subject choices they make as early at age 13, are key contributory factors to the numbers of skilled UK scientists and engineers in the future.

There are particular issues in England. Engineering graduates, for whom A-levels in maths and physics are seen as pre-requisites to studying engineering at higher education, are more likely to have taken three sciences separately at GCSE than core (plus additional) science. The Department for Education's report into maths and science A-level high achievers underlines this link, stating that,

> *"Taking separate science GCSEs increases the chances of taking A-level science qualifications compared with 'core' science GCSEs (the association between separate sciences and A-level entry was strongest for physics, at almost 3 times the odds of pupils who took 'additional' science).[3]"*

1 EngineeringUK (2010) Engineering UK Report 2011

2 EngineeringUK (2009) Engineering UK Report 2009-10 http://www.engineeringuk.com/what_we_do/education_&_research/engineering_uk_2009/10.cfm [Accessed 15.04.11]

3 DfE (2011) http://www.education.gov.uk/publications/RSG/AllPublications/Page1/DFE-RR079 [Accessed 15.04.11]

At age 16, a future engineering graduate generally chooses to study maths *and* physics at A-level. Entry for almost all university engineering degrees requires this combination, and analysis of UCAS applications data by the Institute of Physics showed that, of applications to the ten most popular subject areas for students with both maths and physics A-levels, 45.8% were for engineering courses. Not one student with just maths or just physics A-level applied.

The majority of young people, however, are effectively ruling themselves out of engineering degree courses at age 13-14. Analysis of the 2008 Joint Council for Qualifications (JCQ) qualifications data, shows that amongst all students studying for GCSEs, only 11.7% of boys and 8.7% of girls are studying GCSE physics. Two years later the percentage of boys studying A-level physics, as a proportion of all GCSE students in 2008, was 6.6%. For girls this dropped to 1.8%, meaning that 98.2% of girls had effectively ruled themselves out of studying engineering as a degree. In Scotland the broader curriculum leads to 12.9% of girls studying physics at Standard Grade and 8.5% at Higher Level or Advanced Higher Level, a proportion which is almost 5 times more than in England, Wales and Northern Ireland.

If we look into these statistics a little further, the need to improve young people's perceptions of STEM and careers in STEM, in order to keep their options open, becomes clear. Evidence suggests that young people's enjoyment of a subject is as significant as their attainment in terms of their likelihood to pursue it further. Yet while pupils in the UK have been reported as having comparatively high levels of academic attainment and proficiency levels in science; they have relatively low levels of enjoyment, with girls' enjoyment levels ranking significantly lower than boys'.[4] A major reason why children and young people give up science and maths is a lack of enjoyment and interest, with children in the UK becoming less positive towards these subjects in recent years compared to children in other countries.[5] The "Year 8 Dip" in pupils' motivation and performance is most evident in more traditional academic subjects, including science and maths, yet the following year, these students will be making decisions about their GCSEs that will shape their future studies and careers.

Enquiry-based learning as an approach to overcoming these issues of perception at critical points in a student's school life shows some clear benefits: students are more engaged with the subject, perceive it as more relevant to their own needs, and are enthusiastic and ready to learn. Following their own research interests and allowing students to develop a more flexible approach to their studies, with the freedom and

---

4   OECD 2007: PISA 2006 Science competencies for tomorrows' world Volume 1, Volume 2, Data and Analysis: Paris

5   Educating the next generation of scientists: House of Commons Committee of Public Accounts

responsibility for what and how they learn, helps make subjects more relevant to them, leading to the development of original thought and ideas. Longer term, the skills gained working with and communicating to a group, are key to students' future employability in an increasingly 'knowledge-based' society.

Recognising these benefits, EngineeringUK, through effective partnerships with business, education, third sector and government has, over the last two years, refocused its efforts on providing young people with just these sorts of hands-on opportunities to learn. This is coupled with useful careers information which, together with our traditional and digital media campaigns, are designed to change young people's perceptions of science and engineering. *The Big Bang UK Young Scientists and Engineers Fair* incorporates an annual national event, a series of regional and local fairs, and features the finals of the National Science & Engineering Competition. The biggest event of its kind in the UK, The Big Bang celebrates and raises the profile of young people's achievement in science and engineering, encouraging more young people to see where STEM might take them, with support from their parents and teachers. *Tomorrow's Engineers*, another EngineeringUK programme, provides targeted, high quality, and consistently evaluated enhancement and enrichment activities, featuring project-based learning opportunities and relevant hands-on experience. This is all underpinned by robust STEM careers information provision.

The indications are that this approach to enabling young people to experience science and engineering is working. Young people visiting this year's Big Bang told us the event inspired them (86%), taught them something new about engineering (85%) and 24% of them said they were now "much more likely to want to become an engineer".

The imperative to encourage young people to study STEM subjects is clear: they, and not us, will be responsible for helping to harness future technological advances which will address grand challenges such as climate change, ageing populations, food scarcity, clean water, security and infrastructure renewal, thereby helping businesses to create new jobs, rebalance the UK economy and ensure we remain a key engineering and manufacturing global player. If, however, young people continue to rule themselves out of an engineering degree by the age of 14, the pipeline of future engineers, and ultimately the country as a whole, will lose out. The importance of identifying and developing effective ways to ensure the health of the 'STEM pipeline' of future engineers, by encouraging young people to keep their options open, has never been greater.

Is now the time to challenge the traditional thinking behind a relatively narrow A-level curriculum, embracing genuine enquiry-based learning and vocational routes, to lay the foundations for effective higher education provision in engineering? One thing is certain, if we just keep doing things the same way, we'll keep getting the same results.

Paul Jackson is the Chief Executive of EngineeringUK, a Chartered Engineer and Fellow of the Institution of Engineering and Technology.

EngineeringUK *is an independent, not-for-profit organisation that promotes the vital contribution that engineers, and engineering and technology, make to society.*

The students of tomorrow

Aaron Porter

For those of you watching the recent debate on English higher education funding on our TV screens and on the front pages of our newspapers, you could be forgiven for thinking that higher education was predominantly made up of full-time undergraduates, largely aged between 18-22. Of course that is not the case, and is increasingly less likely to be the case as we start to get under the skin of an ever-changing and diverse higher education population.

Already the picture presented to us by the Higher Education Statistics Agency (HESA) shows us that around 4 in 10 students are part-time, 1 in 5 are postgraduates, and just under 1 in 10 are studying in a further education (FE) college. Putting to one side your opinion on the recent finance reforms – the debate is well-rehearsed – and making an educated guess about what may be in the Government's higher education White Paper, we can be sure that the reforms are almost certainly going to lead to less traditional provision, and even more diversity.

As greater power is put in the hands of the future student, they are likely to choose to learn in different ways and at different times, and are almost certainly going to have different expectations to the students of today. In a speech just before the vote in Parliament on raising the tuition fee cap, I warned that students would likely bring about a "consumer revolution", and whilst I feel incredibly uncomfortable about the idea of 'students as consumers', they will undoubtedly be more demanding about the experience they are likely to receive in the future.

So I suspect as the recent reforms take root, we might start to see an increasingly challenge to the current provision of higher education. The introduction of loans for around two thirds of part-time students is long overdue and welcome, and I hope that it will allow for more part-time students to study alongside part-time work. The pressure to enter full-time higher education at 18 years old will hopefully lessen, as the opportunity to study part-time later in life or even at 18 will now be more viable. And whilst both Browne and the Government missed the opportunity to really seize the mantle and deliver a funding system built on credit, the White Paper will have to address the issue of allowing students to move between and within institutions. The current system has been far too inflexible, not allowing a student to pick up credits over time, as would be possible in a system genuinely based on lifelong learning. Whilst I do not think Lord Browne nor the Government addressed this seriously enough, students will start to demand this in their actions. The idea of students increasingly spending time in different institutions, perhaps for a period as a work-based learner, or switching between full and part-time study, can no longer be prevented, as the student of tomorrow will be increasingly flexible and nimble to respond to the ever-changing demands of the labour market.

It will be the demands of the labour market that will increasingly mean students will want to re-enter higher education later in their working life. As the number of jobs an adult can expect to undertake in their working life continues to spiral upwards, so will the need to re-skill becoming increasingly important. Whilst the traditional campus experience will be important for lots of young adults, access to knowledge and skills will be the greater priority for older learners wanting to upskill or change careers later in life. At present the Open University stands out as the provider of education and qualifications to help the older learner change direction or reskill, but this will need to become the preserve of many more providers, as the UK seeks to keep its adult population with the required skills, and the UK economy competitive with our global competition.

And with an increasingly diverse pattern of provision demanded by future students, they will also have increased expectations of what they will receive too. In our own research NUS/HSBC Student Experience Research 2010;

> "65% of students said that they would have higher expectations if they were being asked to pay considerably more for their education."

Students, then as graduates, are not only being asked to pay considerably more for their higher education, whilst the government savagely cuts the teaching grant, the disastrously handled debate by Vince Cable and the government means that prospective students will be weighing up their options with real scrutiny, but also with concern about what the returns on their investment may be. With the jobs market still so bleak, and so many of the jobs that graduates went into employment with, such as the public sector, being savagely trimmed back, many students will be exerting their consumer traits onto universities with greater force than before.

The gauntlet has been well and truly laid down. In a new environment, with power in the 'hands of students' as David Willetts is so keen to remind us, then universities will need to respond. It can no longer be acceptable that student complaints are left to swill around the system for more than 60 days, at present some are still left unresolved for more than a year. The role of the personal tutor will become more important, as students will want and expect more personalised support to guide them through their learning. The quantity and quality of contact time, which has increasingly come under the spotlight will be an issue of even greater focus. The days when high profile academics are splashed around the university prospectus material, but then hidden away in a research lab away from undergraduate students will no longer be tolerated. Student-led protests against their perceived poor contact time, notably at Bristol and Manchester Universities will happen with increasing frequency unless institutions can respond, and meet rising expectations.

I have no doubts that improved information will be important both for the prospective and current student. The chance to make a more informed choice about what, where and how to study will be important, and then the chance to measure that against their expectations on arrival will be critical. But to ensure the greatest protection for students, we can not simply allow for market forces to run riot alone. The role of the students' union will become even more important in holding the institution to account, and for the National Union of Students (NUS) to do the same with Government and the sector as a whole. With rights comes responsibility, and in the same way I know that students' unions will be afforded greater powers as a result of the new flow of money through the student, I fully expect and welcome the need for Student Unions (SUs) and the NUS to increasingly base what we say on evidence, to back up our arguments with fact, but also to be more accountable and transparent to students too. The system will need to have greater regulation too in order to protect the student, and this will need to be forthcoming in the White Paper too.

The period ahead for higher education will undoubtedly be one of change. Whether we see a "consumer revolution" time will tell, and if it happens whether it will be for better or worse. But what is for sure is that talking about higher education and its students through the narrow lens of full-time 18-22 undergraduates enjoying the traditional campus experience will be less and less relevant, and it's time we all started to get our heads around the landscape and demography of the new world.

Aaron Porter is the National President of the NUS, serving from 10 June 2010 to 01 July 2011. Previously he was twice elected as the NUS Vice-President (Higher Education) and took leading roles in the University of Leicester Students' Union.

The National Union of Students (NUS) is the national voice of students providing representation and campaigns, aiming to improve the lives of students.

Changing student expectations

Jamie O'Connell

The growing cost of higher education the world over means that the motivations for attending and the expectations of the service received are changing.

In the past year two major events have happened to profoundly influence UK higher education (HE) policy, the impact of which won't be fully felt by students until 2012.

Firstly a Coalition Government, led by the Conservative party, was voted in to power in April 2010. The Conservatives have looked to aggressively reduce the nation's budget deficit and cutting back on public spending has been one of the major tactics deployed. Cuts to the English higher education budget of 40% over four years were announced in a spending review on 20 October 2010.

Secondly in October 2010 an independent review conducted by Lord Browne into the future funding of HE in England was published. The 'Browne review' made recommendations for universities to be able to set their own tuition fee limits with no cap. The intention was that the market would dictate who is happy to pay what.

The government embraced the majority of the recommendations in the Browne review with some amendments. From 2012 English universities will be able to charge up to £9,000 per year for undergraduate courses, keeping the cap but raising it from its current level of £3,290. This was backed by Parliament in December 2010 for England, with other UK nations watching developments closely.

The hole that universities have found in their budgets will be filled by student fees. A student loan from Government will cover these increased tuition fees, one that will be paid back upon graduating and securing work that pays above £21,000 a year.

The rise in fees will lead to a change in student expectations and crucially, for universities, this will also change the criteria on which students evaluate which university and course to attend.

What expectations do students have?

Drop out rates in the UK are at about 8.6%, usually because student expectations of what university will be like are found to be different from the reality they experience when they get there.

When asked in a straw poll on The Student Room 'Why do you want to go to university', three areas were identified, they were:

- A desire for the 'student experience' and independence
- A desire to learn and study something they are passionate about
- An expectation that university will lead to a good, well paid job

The weight given to those three factors will be different for everyone, some want to go to university solely to party, others have a specific vocation in mind and university is a very focussed means to that end. However it is my belief that the weighting of those priorities will change when the new tuition fees come into play from 2012.

The student experience

For many, attending university is their first taste of adult freedom. Confidence and life skills come from moving out of the family home, cooking for yourself and managing a budget.

It is also a great opportunity to meet other like-minded students from diverse backgrounds, people you would never get to meet and learn from in any other situation. Beer is cheap, there are parties, social clubs and communal living – university is fun!

But how much fun will be had when students are paying up to £9,000 a year for the privilege?

Students are going to be acutely aware that they need to make the most of their time at university and there will be more of a focus for all students on performing well academically, both as a self-imposed pressure and inevitably also from parents. In addition, research conducted by The Student Room in December 2010 shows that 80% of prospective students anticipate having to work in a part-time job when they attend university in light of the rise in fees.

This means that the 'student experience' and the fun of attending university could be compromised.

Technology is also changing the student experience. There was a time when students going to university would all but lose contact with their school friends from their home town and contact with family would be limited. In the age of social networking and mobile communication young people will remain in contact continually with their friends, those that stay in their home town to work and those that disperse to other universities. This can be a positive thing for students, ensuring that they keep those relationships. However this level of contact with existing friends could act as a substitute for making new contacts. And when times get tough, when revision bites and when a student is feeling lonely at university there will be a strong pull back to their home town and familiar faces.

Students that have traditionally looked to university for 'the experience' may now look closer to home. To their friends that have money in their pockets and who don't risk losing girlfriends/boyfriends by moving away. It may also lead to studying nearer home, which can also lead to cost savings.

Quality of service

Currently the quality of service that students receive varies greatly between institutes. Depending on the course and institution, you may have wildly differing levels of contact time with a tutor/lecturer per week. In a world where students are paying top dollar for their education they will expect to get not only sufficient contact time, comparable to other institutions and courses, but also to get a good standard of tuition and personalised support from a tutor.

In addition to this students will expect to have quality support services available to them – careers guidance, welfare support, financial support, medical support and emotional support. Currently universities offer very mixed support services and with the cuts in university funding there won't be money available in most cases to improve those services. It is entirely likely that there will be a shortfall in expectations here too.

From my own point of view I believe there is an opportunity for some elements of support services to be offered to secondary and higher education institutions on a national scale. This would ensure high quality and low costs by reducing duplication within institutions. Careers provision springs to mind for example.

Securing employment

Currently UK graduate unemployment is at a 15 year high of 20%. There are so many graduates and so few graduate positions that those within employment are often carrying out low-level work that they are greatly over-qualified for.

The expectation with increasing fees is that fewer people will go to university and those that do go will expect a relevant graduate position when they finish.

Remember graduates will need to start paying back their not-insignificant loans when they earn over £21,000. Not such a problem if you are on a management consultancy fast-track and anticipate earning £40,000 within a year. But for many, in the nonprofit or creative arts industries for instance, whose salaries will languish around the £20,000-25,000 mark, paying back that loan will be a real burden. Some graduates will even be a reluctant to ever declare a salary over £20,000.

Will this also mean that students from low income families that choose to attend top fee-charging universities will only do so if they expect to attain a high-paying job? They will feel unable to study the arts for instance, knowing it may not lead to a top flight salary.

The impact of changing expectations on future applications

The concern with the rise in fees is that students from low income families will be deterred from attending. Alternatives, in the UK at least, are not always clear and schools are often ill-equipped to advise on those alternatives.

What is clear is that students who do decide to go to higher education will be choosing the course and institute with great care. The criteria for that selection changing in line with expectations.

Employability will became a key selection criteria, as will the quality of service. In recognition of this greater level of scrutiny that applicants will demand the UK government has said that every university must provide and make publicly available a 'Key Information Set', or KIS data set, for every HE course in the UK from summer 2012. This data set will allow students to easily compare courses on criteria such as contact time per week, employability stats, student feedback etc. UCAS will be publishing this data as a central source and it will be the quantitative information that students will use to evaluate their HE choices.

Traditionally UK students haven't gone overseas in any great number to study. This is set to change. By broadening their options outside of the UK students will be able to find universities that still don't charge fees, universities that offer high quality services and universities which will offer the chance to broaden your horizons while experiencing a new culture and learning a new language.

For the first time UK universities will be in competition with overseas universities for 'typical' UK students, not just 'top-end' students that may have always deliberated between Cambridge or Berkley.

In summary

In the UK, from 2012, universities will be reliant on the fees paid by students in order to provide core services. Therefore universities will need to become a lot more business and customer orientated. Meeting the expectations of their students and graduates will become crucial to their reputation and long term success.

From a students perspective employability and service quality will become the two main points of differentiation when choosing between comparably priced courses. Institutes will need to demonstrate their credentials in these areas and any additional industry links will be a bonus. Universities offering industry supported degrees for example will have an additional point of differentiation. Lancaster University already offers an Ernst & Young business degree; Anglia Ruskin offers a Harrods sales degree; and there are others. Taken to an extreme I would expect to see privatised, industry funded universities appearing. The feeling is that students intent on getting a job and a high quality experience would welcome this.

For some students looking to get the fulfilling 'student experience', studying overseas may become more attractive. And with student sights set on employment, many industries now have limited opportunities in the UK, making studying and then working overseas more appealing.

The application process for university will better support the changing expectations students have. KIS data, compulsory for every HE course in the UK from 2012, will make the process of choosing a university less hit and miss. Students will be able to easily narrow down their institute and course based upon what is most important to them. Overseas universities would do well to keep an eye on the changing criteria UK students will be using to evaluate HE decisions. If they wish to be considered as a credible alternative they will need to provide the same sorts of information about their courses.

Many students concerned with financing their degree will look for more flexible alternatives such as distance learning or part-time study. Universities and the HE system generally will need to adjust to this demand.

Higher education is changing, the world is getting flatter and students are justifiably becoming more demanding. How many universities already refer to students as 'customers'? It's possibly a scary and unwanted development for many, but none the less is quickly becoming a reality.

Jamie O'Connell is Marketing Director of The Student Room and is responsible for organisation strategy, ensuring the website offers the best possible service and functionality for all students and universities. He feels passionately about the role peer to peer support can play in education.

The Student Room *is the world's largest student web community, with 26 million page views and 3.9 million unique users each month. Members are predominantly young people aged 14-26 who offer support and advice to each other via forums on subjects ranging from study help, going to university and careers to health, music and relationships.*

Section six – How should teaching, learning and assessment evolve?

How to drive quality teaching

Craig Mahoney

The perennial discussion about what constitutes quality in higher education often resides in a debate about teaching. This has been the case recently across the UK and particularly in England, resulting from proposals on future fees and student finance in England.

Teaching is not the be-all and end-all of higher education but it does make the single biggest contribution to the student learning experience and student success. In 2010, the Higher Education Academy (HEA) published a report on the 'dimensions of quality' in higher education by Professor Graham Gibbs.[1] This meta-analysis examined factors that make up a high quality learning experience for students in higher education. Gibbs found that process variables – the way institutions use their resources – make the biggest difference to educational outcomes. He picks out class size, the level of student effort and engagement, who does the teaching, and quality of feedback to students on their work as the significant and valid process indicators.

At the HEA a major concern in this report is on the third of these points – who does the teaching. At present there are very few barriers to becoming a teacher in higher education. Higher education teaching/lecturing is one of very few professions in which people can work with no requirement to have any qualification or licence to practice – although increasingly universities do require staff, new to teaching, to be trained. Students go to university to learn, and good teaching is integral to effective learning. But at present there is no formal requirement that those who teach students in higher education should hold a teaching qualification or be qualified to teach.

I have long argued that staff who have undertaken training and professional development in teaching in higher education are better equipped to support and inspire their students. They also have greater self awareness of the subtle factors impacting the learning environment such as psychology, philosophy and sociology of learning. Professional development leading to professional recognition provides a benchmark for individuals and for institutions, and more importantly gives the general population and students themselves confidence that they are being supported by

1   http://www.heacademy.ac.uk/news/detail/dimensions_of_quality_report [Accessed 15.04.11]

qualified, capable and competent professionals. My experience is that individuals who are qualified are better prepared, more knowledgeable and have a better grasp on the demands from teaching to provide a quality teaching experience that students do, and increasingly will, expect. The research evidence in this area is limited for higher education though considerable evidence exists for the positive impact on student learning from qualified teachers in secondary education.

This topic continues to provoke strong reactions in which Institutions argue, rightly so, that they must have the autonomy to manage and develop their staff for their own institutional circumstances. The UK Professional Standards Framework, (UKPSF) provides a UK-wide set of descriptors, developed with the higher education sector, against which institutions can benchmark their approaches to the professional development of staff. It is managed by the HEA on behalf of the sector, and offers universities and colleges criteria which support the initial and continuing professional development for staff who teach and support student learning. Academics can show how their teaching is informed by research and by professional practice. It is a flexible framework that is adaptable to the needs of the individual and of the institution. The framework is unique and is gaining increased recognition internationally.

Many institutions use the UKPSF and seek external validation of their approaches to professional development against the framework. The HEA alone accredits 378 programmes in 140 higher education institutions across the UK. The UKPSF is not, and was never intended to be, mandatory. There are other routes to accreditation too, which the HEA welcomes.

Clearly, provision varies across the sector in terms of the length, content and credit rating of programmes, as well as their alignment against the UKSPF. Also not all institutions require academic staff who are new to teaching to undertake a Post Graduate Certificate in Higher Education (PGCE) or equivalent. Even where institutions have a formal requirement, it may not always be enforced. Moreover, it is not uncommon for research activity and associated outcomes to be prioritised ahead of the development of knowledge and pedagogy related to teaching.

In November 2010, the HEA launched a review of the UKPSF in consultation with the higher education sector. The HEA found broad general support for the principle that those who teach in higher education should be appropriately qualified. What is ripe for debate is how this might operate in practice. The HEA does not espouse a one size fits all approach and accepts concerns in the sector that acknowledging mission differences, diversity of provision and institutional autonomy are crucial in reaching agreement on how any revised framework should operate. Nevertheless, the UKPSF, with its origins and ownership in the sector, has the potential to be a key indicator of UK higher education's ongoing commitment to teaching and supporting learning, as well as giving confidence that minimum threshold standards have been met by academic staff.

The second part of the debate on higher education teaching relates to the manner in which teaching can be properly recognised in institutional reward and promotions policies. The dominance of research over teaching may appear endemic both in the culture of many universities and in formal processes, like academic promotion policies. In 2008, a collaborative project by the HEA and Professor Annette Cashmore at the University of Leicester's GENIE Centre for Excellence in Teaching and Learning, found that despite the vital role that teaching plays in a student's experience of university, research performance remains more central in most university promotion policies for academics.[2]

In reviewing the UKPSF and in order to stimulate sector-wide debate, the HEA put forward potential guidelines that higher education institutions might consider when developing their promotions criteria based on teaching. While individual organisations emphasised the need for institutional autonomy, the presentation of potential indicators was welcomed. There is general agreement that support in this area is best provided though the sharing of good practice and the provision of supportive guidance material.

In the future higher education teaching qualifications need to be reviewed as part of a package of measures that help raise the status of teaching – although this may seem a hugely difficult task at a time when funding for teaching, across the UK, is under review. However, with 2.4 million students enrolled in UK higher education, the work that lecturers put in to supporting students' learning is something that all of us must take more seriously and respond to appropriately as expectations from existing and future student groups rise. This is the best way of ensuring that quality is improved across higher education in the future.

Professor Craig Mahoney is Chief Executive of The Higher Education Academy, is a Chartered Psychologist and was past Chair of the British Association of Sport and Exercise Sciences (BASES).

The Higher Education Academy supports the sector in providing the best possible learning experience for all students.

2   http://www.heacademy.ac.uk/news/detail/2009/rewardandrecongition2 [Accessed 15.04.11]

Learning for the future

Phil Race

It has long been recognised that learning happens by doing rather than by just being in the presence of someone more learned. For centuries, higher education educators' roles centred on transmitting the content of precious books, articles and other resources in ways that learners could handle. Now, information is ubiquitous. Most learning resources are available to just about everyone on-line (often free) or through a plethora of information-handling channels. This necessitates transformed roles for educators, to help learners to prosper and thrive by their own efforts in the sea of information. I argue, however, that in higher education we're not keeping up with our learners, often failing to respond to the questions in their minds, including:

- What am I supposed to be learning here?
- What *else* should I be learning?
- Why am I learning this and why here in this lecture room?
- How best can I learn this successfully?
- How does this fit with all the things I know already?
- With what resources and materials am I supposed to achieve this learning?
- How exactly am I expected to be able to show that I have learned successfully?
- How will my learning be measured, and by whom, where, and when?
- How best can I make sure that I get due credit for my learning?

Teaching: making learning happen

The role of academic staff in higher education is moving fast towards being expert facilitators of learning. The person at the lectern is no more merely a communicator of scholarly information to students, but now needs to help them to navigate successfully through a sea of information on the web, at home, in the workplace, on the go and in libraries and resource centres. More importantly, the crucial role of the teacher is now to design the assessment of learning and accredit evidence of achievement. Learning used to be measured using what came from students' pens in exam rooms and coursework assignments; now assessment spans many other ways in which students evidence their achievement, including presentations, working with fellow-students, reflecting on and self-assessing their work, and critiquing and making judgements on other people's achievements.

Factors underpinning successful learning

Over the last couple of decades, I've asked over 100,000 people questions about how they learn. My findings[1] indicate that seven factors underpin successful learning:

1. *Wanting* to learn – curiosity, and the desire to succeed;

2. *Needing* to learn – having good reasons to learn, taking ownership of targets deemed to show successful learning;

3. Learning by *doing* – practice, repetition, experimenting, trial and error;

4. Learning through *feedback* – praise, critical comments, feedback from fellow-learners and expert tutors;

5. *Making sense* of what is being learned – students say *'getting my head around it'* regarding concepts, theories and models;

6. Deepening learning by *explaining* things to others – practising *communicating* the learning;

7. Further deepening learning by *making judgements* – for example applying criteria to their own work (self-assessment) or to others' work (peer-assessment).

The vital part of the academic's job is now to help learners focus in on these processes. We still need to inspire, motivate and clarify difficult concepts, but gone are the days when it was enough to say to students 'I'll tell you what I know, but then it's your job (and not my responsibility), to work out what to do with what I've provided for you'.

Do we measure the right things?

When it comes to *measuring* learning, too often we still tend to base our judgments on mere written words, setting parameters such as 3,000 word essays, 10,000 word dissertations and 60,000 word theses – strange equivalences are asserted between numbers of words, hours of learning and credit points. The volume of handwritten or typed words alone is seldom a sensible basis for quantifying learning. Every assessment process is (and always has been) just a proxy for measuring what's in students' heads, and what they can do with what's there. We can only measure learning in terms of what students can communicate, but we're now in an age where relatively little human communication happens with pen in hand (when did you last *write* more than a shopping list or post-it note on the fridge?). No wonder that 'handwriting for a

1 For more detail, please see chapter 2 of Race. P. (2010) *Making Learning Happen (2nd edition)* London: Sage

degree' in exams feels like a time-warp to students, constraining and strange, without the possibility of assembling, re-assembling then developing thoughts on-screen in front of them, touch-typing or searching for information online as they go. We need to modernise our assessment tactics to be more online, more digital, more virtual, more face-to-face, more use of social media technologies, and more interactive. We know that assessment drives learning – just ask students. But as long as assessment is predominantly (hand)written, learning in higher education will continue to lag behind other aspects of our advancing civilisation.

Addressing the changing context

Higher education has never before been in such a state of rapid evolution, as highlighted in other chapters. 'Customer satisfaction' and league tables dominate planning, distracting from the most important elements of change, students themselves – and they're changing fast, really fast. Students are becoming more value-conscious, more litigious, more diverse in background, experience and capability, more expectant of academic support, but less tolerant of poor teaching or unfair assessment.

Students today don't come to universities to receive information or sit in lectures being presented with things they could have found faster by themselves. The age of 'reading for a degree' is perhaps over – students are now browsing, skimming, clicking, cutting-and-pasting, editing, drafting and re-drafting for a degree. Students now expect to find what they're looking for in two clicks on their net-books, tablet-computers or smart-phones. If what they find requires payment or registration, they will usually skip it and look elsewhere. Sit among the students in a large lecture and watch what's on their laptops or mobile phone screens; If they're *really* interested, it is possibly the results of web searches related to what the lecturer is talking about. More often, it's Facebook, YouTube or heaven knows what, with no more than half an ear to the lecture. No surprise that the UK National Student Survey (NSS) results often show significant levels of dissatisfaction about the enthusiasm and commitment of teaching staff. In future, the challenge for lecturers is to ensure that every large-group session is something quite special – an important ingredient in the recipe for student learning.

Learning for the future

Long gone are the days when all a lecturer needed was mastery of relevant subject matter, and it mattered little how well learning was facilitated. Students are ever more likely to walk away literally or metaphorically from an unsatisfactory learning experience, or make their dissatisfaction very clear in evaluations. Practitioners in higher education need to be able to 'cause learning to happen', and measure evidence of students' achievement. The processes of teaching, and designing assessment are now much more important than the mere 'delivery' of subject content. Institutions – and educators – who fail to acknowledge this will face a precarious future.

Phil Race is Visiting Professor at the University of Plymouth, and Emeritus Professor of Leeds Metropolitan University. He publishes widely on teaching, learning and assessment. More information can be found on his website at www.phil-race.co.uk.

The purpose and process of lifelong learning: all work and no play?

Ezri Carlebach

The term 'lifelong learning' has its modern origins in post World War I reconstruction efforts. In view of the extension of suffrage, and with a least one eye on the principles of the October Revolution in Russia, the Adult Education Committee of the Ministry of Reconstruction declared in 1919 that;

> *"adult education… is a permanent national necessity, an inseparable aspect of citizenship, and therefore should be both universal and lifelong".*[1]

The use of lifelong learning as a policy term took recognisable shape in the 1970s with the arrival of the 'knowledge economy' as a driver of education and skills thinking, soon followed by the creation of a 'learning society' as a pan-political aspiration.

Lifelong learning in the sense I intend it here extends across a range of different settings, whether in the workplace, in a youth group, at a local library or community centre, or in a college, institute or university. It also stretches from some point in life at around 14 years through – if demographic predictions are to be believed – to 114 years, covering the various milestones that can occur in a person's life such as parenthood, career change, relocation and so on.

Lifelong learning builds innovation

As Will Hutton recently pointed out, the competitiveness of the UK depends on the promulgation of a "learning culture" that will support the knowledge economy. To achieve that, we need highly skilled and adaptable workers who can fill the jobs that are now, and will be increasingly, dependent on higher-order thinking and creative abilities. Hutton posits lifelong learning as;

> *"part of Britain's emergent innovation architecture".*[2]

If we truly believe in lifelong learning, the knowledge economy and a learning society, then we need a system that reduces rather than emphasises differences between the process and experience of learning in the different settings and life stages alluded to above. While it will continue to be the case for most young people making choices at

---

1 Quoted in John Field, 'Lifelong Education', *International Journal of Lifelong Education*, 20: 1, 3–15, 2001.

2 Keynote speech, Lifelong Learning UK annual conference, 8 December 2009.

14 or thereabouts that there are broad variations in possible pathways, there needs to be considerably more weight given to choices that extend options rather than reduce them.

Speaking at the 2011 Owers Lecture[3] Peter Mitchell, chief executive of the Baker Dearing Educational Trust, highlighted the need for better progression planning right through the education system, planning that involves employers much more effectively and that is based on encouraging learners to "leave doors open".

The University Technical Colleges (UTCs) that the Baker Dearing Trust is now promoting, and which the Coalition government has pledged to support, hold out the promise of a more 'open-doors' approach in the critical 14-19 space. The UTCs are based on partnerships between universities, colleges of further education, local authorities and employers. The universities contribute, among other things, curriculum development, support and mentoring for students – including pathways into degree courses – and expertise in information and research skills.

Work, learn and play

These things, the current orthodoxy asserts, all contribute to employability, encourage aspiration and provide a platform for a future commitment to learning, retraining, reskilling and so on. But it is precisely in the 14-19 age range, when young people make extraordinary leaps in their physical, emotional and intellectual growth, that our system tends to marginalise specific attributes and attitudes that are, in fact, essential to the desired employment and economic outcomes.

These attributes and attitudes are found in play more readily than in either learning or work. The video games industry often comes up as an exemplar of modern design and manufacturing in which the UK leads the world. It seems we have no problem with play as a factor driving *consumption* of goods and services, but we don't sufficiently appreciate or encourage its importance to *production* – and therefore wealth creation – whether in the technical or business realms.

This is of course because play is seen as the realm of the very young or of those at leisure, and thus the opposite of work, whilst at the same time work itself has become an all-encompassing realm, as indicated by the shift in Sunday supplement-speak from 'work-life balance' to 'work-life blend'. Some may argue that 'life' here includes play, but not, I would suggest, in the specific manner in which play is important to lifelong learning and its economic consequences.

---

3   The University Technical College: A basis for a manufacturing renaissance? 24 March 2011

In his classic work on the primary role of play in creating human culture, Dutch historian Johan Huizinga wrote;

> "[t]o dare, to take risks, to bear uncertainty, to endure tension – these are the essence of the play spirit".[4]

They are also the hallmarks of effective lifelong learning and at the same time characterise the very employability skills most needed by successful modern knowledge workers and their employers.

Rousseau spoke of "the most useful of all arts, the art of training men".[5] The current political climate demands that those providing publicly supported lifelong learning must prove their usefulness; i.e. that they deliver value for money to 'UK Plc' in the form of jobs and/or wealth created, whilst apparently granting less credence to the role of 'arts' in those accomplishments. As Hutton again points out, it was the knowledge economy, particularly the creative industries, that led Britain out of recession in the 1980s and 1990s, and it is likely that they will lead Britain out of its current woes.

The question that remains for anyone concerned with the learning supply side is what impact does this economic imperative for lifelong learning have on our practice and our values as a learner- and learning-driven sector? It is important to observe that not only are those values not at odds with the economic priorities of a post-recessionary environment, but they are actually fundamentally important to recovery and growth. We must also beware that the economic imperative does not drive out the play spirit that is, in fact, at the heart of our ability to overcome technological, economic and social challenges.

Ezri Carlebach *was Communications & Research Director at* Lifelong Learning UK, *the sector skills council for post-compulsory education employers, until it closed in March 2011. He has previously held senior marketing and communications roles in higher education, the arts and heritage sector and financial services. He now works on a number of strategic communications projects and is completing a Master's in Philosophy at Birkbeck College.*

4   *Homo Ludens,* Boston, MA: Beacon Press, 1950.
5   *Emile,* 1762, Project Gutenberg E-edition, 2004.

First class: how assessment can enhance student learning

Sally Brown

Too many universities pay insufficient attention to assessment: usually the mechanics are adequately managed, but the purposes and practices are less well thought-through, relying on 'tried and tested' approaches, which in reality are neither.

> *'Nothing we do to, or for our students is more important than our assessment of their work and the feedback we give them on it. The results of our assessment influence students for the rest of their lives and careers'.*[1]

Assessment in higher education can be a powerful force, either to help students make sense of their learning, or conversely to make it a negative and demoralising experience. As Boud suggests:

> *"Students can escape bad teaching: they can't escape bad assessment".*[2]

Some would even say that our current assessment system is broken, that nothing less than a radical overhaul can save it from falling into total disrepute. In many universities, time-consuming and expensive complaints often centre on student dissatisfaction with what are sometimes, in truth, poor or even reprehensible university assessment practices. More students and their (fee-paying) parents are taking universities to court, questioning not just the fair implementation of assessment processes, but also the academic judgments on which grades are based.

So how can we use assessment as a force to positively enhance the student experience? We can direct students' learning behaviours by designing and implementing better assessment. Students often treat marks like money:

> *"How much is it worth? How much time should I spend on this?"*

So if we want to steer their behaviour towards deeper learning approaches, we need to improve assignments.

If we *really* want students to leave everything to the last minute, cut-and-paste, plagiarise and regurgitate memorised material, we should set them tasks that reward such behaviour (as many off-the-shelf essay and exam questions do), but if we want

---

1   Race, P., Brown, S. and Smith, B. (2005) 500 Tips on assessment: 2nd edition, London: Routledge.,.
2   Boud, D. (1995) Enhancing learning through self-assessment London: Routledge.

them to genuinely engage with assessment, we must offer assignments that require incremental submission of work, feature personal research and demonstrate original thinking, while applying theory to practice in authentic contexts.

Assignments should model the practices that graduates will need in real life, demonstrating their skills as historians, scientists or health practitioners, rather than over-relying on essays, where 'writing about' is used as a proxy for 'knowing'. Too often we assess what is easy to assess rather than focusing on the heart of what students need to know and do.[3]

The following are my evidence-based observations which could help guide improvements in assessment practice:

Assessment should be an integral part of the learning process

There have been recent moves away from the expectation that assessment is (just) *of* learning to agreeing that assessment is integral to learning.[4] Well designed assignments require students to both demonstrate their competences and to apply what they have learned to subject-relevant contexts.

Good feedback is essential to student learning

Students benefit from (and expect) timely feedback: the longer students have to wait to get work back, the less likely it is that they will make constructive use of lecturers' comments. This implies that work should be returned very quickly, certainly no more than three working weeks after submission, while the students still care and while there is still time for them to act upon advice.[5]

If we want to set good study patterns, we need to design assignments early in the first year of study that encourage positive learning behaviours

Well-integrated, authentic assessment in the first year that includes a variety of early 'low stakes' assessed tasks can energise and motivate students. The first half of the first semester of the first year is our best opportunity to meaningfully engage them.[6] Early assignments should improve information literacy (crucially including the

---

3   John Biggs' work on 'constructive alignment' emphasises the importance of clarifying at the outset what students need to know and be able to do, and then designing curriculum delivery and assessment around this. See Biggs, J. (2003) Teaching for Quality Learning at University (Maidenhead: SRHE & Open University Press).

4   See http://www.northumbria.ac.uk/sd/central/ar/academy/cetl_afl Biggs, J. (2003) Teaching for Quality Learning at University (Maidenhead: SRHE & Open University Press).

5   Nicol, D. J. and Macfarlane-Dick, D. (2006) Formative assessment and self-regulated learning: A model and seven principles of good feedback practice. Studies in Higher Education, Vol 31(2), 199-218

6   See Yorke, M. (1999) Leaving Early: Undergraduate Non-completion in Higher Education, London: Routledge.

ability to identify which are trustworthy web-derived texts), effective referencing of sources, appropriate academic conduct (many plagiarists, who readily download music and images without a thought for copyright, don't understand the concept of acknowledging sources) and conventions of academic writing (for example, to what extent is a passive third-person voice required?). Too little, too much or the wrong kind of assessment can impact negatively, particularly on students already at risk of failure, withdrawal or underperformance.

Diverse assessment methods and approaches can benefit all students

Most universities use three dominant assessment methods: unseen, time-constrained exams, reports and essays. But if we over-use a small subset of available methods, the same students are disadvantaged time and time again. If instead we offer a mixed diet, students who excel at oral presentations, essay writing, problem solving, group work and so on, can all have their place in the sun.

International students studying in a global environment are likely to need inducting into local assessment practices

There are significant variations between systems, for example in the size and scope of assignments, the amount of oral assessment used (common in Scandinavia and the Netherlands), the level or formality expected in written work, the extent to which assessed group work is acceptable (not permitted in Denmark) and the extent to which Multiple Choice Tests are used.[7] In a competitive international HE market, we ignore at our peril the significant differences in assessment expectations of international students.

We massively under-use technologies that deliver assessments and manage the results

Many nations make much wider use than the UK of the increasingly sophisticated computer-based methods for removing the drudgery of routine marking. A whole range of question types can be used, including menu-driven drag-and-drop questions, interactive maps, graphs, dashboards and free-text responses, all of which go well beyond Multiple-Choice questions.

Individual routes through computer-based assessment programmes can be part of the learning process, with students being given guidance on why right or wrong answers are so, and being given further chances to answer parallel questions until learning is demonstrated. This can be a very cost-effective way of personalising learning.

---

7   See for example chapter 5 in Jones, E. and Brown, S. (2007) Internationalising higher education, London: Routledge, and Ryan, J. (2000) A Guide to Teaching International Students Oxford Centre for Staff and Learning Development.

Many are excited by the potential for computer assessment of essays and other forms of free text. While some claim this is already possible, I believe that currently we can only really recognise word strings, but developing work on computer-based parsing language can determine whether those word strings appear in grammatical sentences. Today, the best we can do is approximate assessment of short answer questions, but this is a new technological field and one that is developing fast.[8]

Technologies are also invaluable for managing personal data: for example, most universities now support e-Portfolios to enable students to provide flexible and accessible evidence of their employability competences, developed both within the university setting and elsewhere, including volunteering, university societies, and part-time work.[9]

At the same time, efficient and innovative data management systems can help compile and correlate marks, link them to the learning outcomes in course documentation, map them to quality assurance benchmarks, as well as to professional and subject body requirements, and enable individual student progression to be tracked and recorded.[10]

Conclusions

I predict that universities of the future will be less concerned about content delivery, since students can access diverse information ubiquitously, and will focus more closely on the recognition and accreditation of learning, wherever that might have taken place (in the workplace, in different national contexts and using open source materials). This means that we need to concentrate more strongly on supporting student engagement with learning, and I argue that the strongest locus of this is through improving assessment.

Sally Brown is Emeritus Professor at Leeds Metropolitan University where she was Pro-Vice-Chancellor (Academic), Adjunct professor at the University of the Sunshine Coast, Queensland and Visiting Professor at the University of Plymouth.

8   See Guest, E. and Brown, S., (2007) A new method for parsing student text to support computer assisted assessment of free text answers, in: Khandia, F. (ed.) 11th CAA International Computer Assisted Conference: Proceedings of the Conference on 10th & 11th July 2007 at Loughborough University, Loughborough, pp. 223-236.

9   JISC (2010) Effective Assessment in a Digital Age HEFCE Bristol provides information about HEIs using e-Portfolios and many useful examples of how assessment can be supported through technologies

10   See http://www.taskstream.com/pub/uk/welcometotaskstream.pdf

Section seven – What should the role of enterprise and business be?

Innovation in higher education

Geoff Mulgan and Mary Abdo

For universities around the world these are both exhilarating and troubling times. Enrolment in tertiary education has risen beyond any expectations, to some 150m[1] worldwide. A truly global industry has taken shape – with new technology enabling rapid collaboration and dissemination of ideas, and students increasingly matriculating at foreign institutions.

Yet there is also disquiet. Much important knowledge creation takes place outside of higher education. Few institutions are rich or self-sustaining, and many face severe squeezes on costs. Despite high hopes, only a handful have actually made a surplus from their technology transfer and spin-out activities.

So what might universities become in an era which should be so rich in opportunity? It would be strange if the same answer was right for all universities, given the diverse needs of university stakeholders, which include students, governments, industry, and academics. Many higher education institutions have tried to be all things to all people, and a few institutions at the top can do this effectively. But most fail. That's why we believe the key to the future of higher education lies elsewhere: in greater pluralism, with the deliberate cultivation of diverse models; in greater specialisation, with universities identifying a few areas in which they will excel; and in better integration, with institutions and individuals sharing knowledge more effectively but also integrating more effectively with the world outside. In what follows we suggest how these goals may be realised.

HE institutions need to innovate as they become both more global and more local

Foreign HE systems, particularly in Asia, are growing at exceptional pace: India aims to build 800-1000 new universities[2] and many upwardly mobile foreign students are now attending university, with China's students already comprising 14% of the international student population. Many English-language universities are setting up new campuses

---

1 UNESCO (2009): Trends in Global Higher Education: Tracking an Academic Revolution: A Report Prepared for the UNESCO 2009 World Conference on Higher Education. Paris: UNESCO. Available at: http://unesdoc.unesco.org/images/0018/001831/183168e.pdf

2 800 varsities, 35,000 colleges needed in next 10 years: Sibal". The Hindu. 24 March 2010.

abroad, while some foreign institutions (like Nankai University in Tianjin, China) are attracting cost-conscious Western students with the promise of low prices. And some countries are building up comparative advantage: Australia, with barely 0.3% of the world's population, boasts 7% of all international students. Britain is in on the game too: in 2010, then-Prime Minister Gordon Brown suggested that in 10 years HE would be "Britain's biggest export"[3]. But some universities need to pursue an opposite strategy: becoming more embedded in their local communities and economies, encouraging students to study near home. And some must do both at once. A good example is Adelaide's University City: Adelaide has imported foreign excellence, including offshoots of Carnegie Mellon and UCL, but has also encouraged its universities to become tightly enmeshed in the regional economy. Other places aiming for a similar result include Guangzhou University City which aims to have 200,000 students and 20,000 academic staff, and Singapore, which is attracting foreign talent to research hubs such as its Biopolis, a state-of-the-art biomedical research centre.

Higher education needs to innovate and evolve both technologies and 'face to face' interactions

It has been 40 years since the Open University provided a fully-formed alternative to the traditional university. The University of Phoenix in the US (and expanding) has pioneered a cost-conscious, scalable alternative too (albeit with many critics of the quality of what's achieved). Online platforms like iTunes U, TED and eduFire now enable everyone to enjoy the best lectures worldwide free of charge. Yet it's remarkable how little technology has changed university education. Few institutions capitalise on technology to improve teaching, and fewer use it to join up efforts across institutions. The National Center for Academic Transformation in the US incentivised institutions to experiment with new ways of teaching using technology; on average institutions cut costs by 39% with improved pass rates and student satisfaction. However, the very ease of access to technology reinforces how important face-to-face interaction remains. In every creative industry, contrary to expectations, consumption of electronic forms has risen in tandem with consumption of the live direct experience, albeit often with creative new forms of live and face to face experience. Peter Drucker forecast that by the 2020s "the big university campuses will be relics". But his prediction is likely to turn out to be as wrong as similar forecasts that told of the demise of the concert and the football match.

Higher education needs to innovate so that it becomes part of all stages of life

With more mature students (the university population of over-25s increased by 15.3% between 2007-08 and 2008-09)[4], we should expect universities to offer courses

---

3   Gordon Brown speech, Kings Cross Hub, April 2010.

4   Eason, G. "Record applicants accepted at UK universities in 2009". BBC News. 21 January 2010.

for mid-career top-ups and for career switches. More programmes like Harvard's Advanced Leadership Initiative pilot, which "challenges the concept of retirement", may crop up, offering individuals the opportunity to retrain as well as to share their insights with younger students. Perhaps too we will see more integration of learning and work at all stages. This approach has always been the aim of law, medicine, and military academies. The idea that you learn best by applying knowledge and that the best teachers are also practitioners is not inherently alien to higher education, and it is almost certainly becoming more relevant to business, particularly in a service economy. Moreover, the soft skills of collaboration, team work, entrepreneurship and communication are best learned through practice – not just through pedagogy.

HE institutions will need to innovate to cut costs

In the UK, at least, HE institutions will receive less money from government. A drop in revenues need not, however, always mean passing on the cost to students in the form of higher fees. There are many interesting examples of alternative means of cutting costs or offsetting student loans – from South Africa's CIDA, where students had to help with cooking, cleaning, and maintenance to keep costs down to the widespread US Federal Work Study Programme, which allows students to offset loans by working in campus offices. Attention to costs is also likely to encourage partnerships and sharing. The Scottish Universities Physics Alliance is an early leader, joining up research efforts across institutions to share resources, cultivate areas of excellence and avoid duplication. Another radical example is researchbase.eu, a platform for collaboration among Europe's best researchers, being developed under the banner of Atomium Culture by the creator of a key underlying technology for Google, Massimo Marchiori.

HE institutions will need to innovate to lower barriers to participation

No-one knows what the optimal proportion of the population passing through HE is (and of course it depends very much on what HE actually provides and is intended to accomplish). But more dynamic economies probably do require a greater supply of well-educated graduates. The Open University, already a leader in open access to HE, has a promising model for making courses even more accessible; in 2006 it launched OpenLearn, making a growing selection of distance learning course materials available for free access, including downloadable versions for educators to modify, plus free collaborative learning-support tools. Another good example is a project at the National University of the Northwest of Buenos Aires Province (UNNOBA), which, in a response to rapid demographic change, engages people of retirement age who return to study.

These are just a few of a spectrum of innovative options that show how HE could become more diverse, and therefore better able to respond to a range of conflicting pressures. But the oddity of our present HE systems around the world is that there is little attention to innovation in how higher education is organised. There are some good reasons for the conservatism of institutions, for their emphasis on research, and for the cultural and social signifiers of mortar boards, gowns and scrolls. But it's easy to forget how recent the current forms are. Cardinal Newman – so influential in shaping ideas of the university in the 19th century – believed that training the intellect through the acquisition of universal knowledge was the only role of the university, and he saw research, as Balliol's Benjamin Jowett put it, as *"a mere excuse for idleness"* which had no place in the university.

The current forms of the university are certainly not eternal. Yet radical innovation is rare. There are a few exceptions like Aalto University in Finland, or the radically reshaped course structure of Melbourne University. But systematic innovation has never been deliberately cultivated. Yet this is almost certainly what we need now: more deliberate innovation to cultivate a more diverse HE landscape better suited to the complex needs of a modern society.

Geoff Mulgan is currently the Chief Executive of the Young Foundation and will become the new Chief Executive of NESTA in June 2011. Some of his previous roles include; Director of Tony Blair's Strategy Unit, Founder and Director of the think-tank Demos, Chief Adviser to Gordon Brown MP, a lecturer in telecommunications, an investment executive, and a reporter on BBC TV and radio. He is a visiting professor at LSE, UCL and Melbourne University.

Mary Abdo is the Project Lead on the Citizens' University at the Young Foundation. Previously, Mary was the Practice Lead for Youth Transitions, with responsibility for The Youth of Today. Before that she was a consultant with McKinsey spin-off Portas Consulting and a Director at a Los Angeles literacy programme Reading to Kids. Mary has a Masters of Public Policy from Harvard.

The Young Foundation brings together insights, innovation and entrepreneurship to meet social needs. It has a track record of over 50 years success with ventures such as the Open University, Which?, the School for Social Entrepreneurs and Healthline (the precursor of NHS Direct). It works across the UK and internationally – carrying out research, influencing policy, creating new organisations and supporting others to do the same, often with imaginative uses of new technology.

It now has over 60 staff, working on over 40 ventures at any one time, with staff in New York and Paris as well as London and Birmingham in the UK.

How higher education can drive an enterprise revolution

Wendy Purcell and Caroline Chipperfield

Universities are places of discovery and innovation, as expressed through the two pillars of their activities; teaching and research. Around the world some universities are moving to view their academic endeavours through the lens of enterprise, further extending their so-called 'third stream' activity and embracing a wider cultural and social agenda. From this perspective;

> "*being enterprising is the ability to respond to change, take risks, to innovate and to generate and implement new ideas and new ways of doing things. Put simply, enterprise is having ideas and making them happen.*"[1]

In this way enterprise draws upon both teaching and research, creating value by delivering learning that enjoys currency, social responsibility and high employability as well as research that reflects societal impact, application and innovation[2].

In the UK, there has been a long tradition of 'civic universities'. These universities were developed in the nineteenth Century by entrepreneurs and civic leaders to satisfy a strong social imperative and the changing demands placed on cities for an increasingly skilled workforce.

However, a new paradigm is emerging – going beyond that of a civic university – the enterprise university. As Goddard notes:

> "*a wider view of the economic and social role of universities, going far beyond technology and skills transfer, is developing and should be encouraged*"[3]

This new model university maintains its strong commitment to knowledge dissemination, creation and transfer, but pursues its mission in partnership in order to sustain and enrich its academic offer. These universities, bold and entrepreneurial, are beginning to accelerate this change, placing more emphasis on their role as an 'urban innovation engine'[4] and increasingly recognised as significant anchor institutions with an important presence within a city and community[5].

1   HEFCE 2010

2   Vorley, T. and Nelles, Jen. 2008. (Re)Conceptualising the Academy: Institutional development of and beyond the third Mission. OECD. December 2008

3   Goddard, J. Reinventing the Civic University. NESTA 2010

4   Williams, L. Turner, N. and Jones A. 2008. The Work Foundation - Embedding Universities in Knowledge Cities. December 2008

5   The Work Foundation.2010. Research Paper 2 Anchoring Growth: The role of 'Anchor Institutions' in the regeneration of UK cities. January 2010

Universities attract smart and creative people; innovate through practice, development and commercialisation. They also contain a range of unique facilities and are able to reach out and build strong networks of partners that can drive social inclusion and economic growth.

The culture that underpins successful enterprise endeavour

At the core of an enterprise university is the development of an enterprise enabling and sustaining culture. For many universities, this requires a distinct step-change in thinking; from an organisation based solely on its excellence in basic research and focus on personal learning, to one where innovation and engagement is embedded, actively shaping the university's offer through team working and partnership.

In many cases, the successful establishment of an enterprise culture is a genuine change of emphasis and requires a new model of leadership, shifting away from 'command and control' to one that embraces 'learn and adapt' behaviours. An enterprise culture relies upon an agility where confidence in ideas and risk-sharing are encouraged, actively championed and rewarded. This in turn empowers staff and fosters innovation in order to create an environment in which the organisation can excel.

Change agents

As Kotter[6] describes, it is important in any change programme to secure early indicators of success – the so-called 'quick wins'. This builds confidence in the organisation and supports the generation of new ideas, accelerating the pace of change and encouraging others to engage. One way of accelerating change is through an 'enterprise enablers' programme. These comprise staff from a range of levels and roles, working together to create small steps of change in their own departments and teams, in line with delivery against the overall institutional mission.

These agents of change are the enthusiasts, the early adopters and those of a more cynical tone who wanted to get on with 'doing enterprise'. They act as catalysts to accelerate and develop the mission, promoting the agenda at a more local level – translating corporate intent into individual delivery. They are also key to the 'sense making' necessary for individuals at the local level to interpret, understand and adopt change.

Academics – tackling cultural change head-on

At the root of a university enterprise culture is a core belief that all members of staff and indeed the entire student body can be enterprising – in particular in championing

6   Kotter John P. 1995. Leading Change: Why Transformation Efforts Fail. Harvard Business Review. March–April 1995

the role of creativity and innovation to tackle challenges head on. AIM Research in 2010[7] showed that academics are five times as entrepreneurial as the general public but often do not consider themselves in this way. Perkmann and Salter highlighted that academics believe that institutions do not value their

"*entrepreneurial activities and that these activities count little in the promotion and recruitment decisions of their universities*".[8]

For a successful enterprise culture it is important that the pathways to reward and career progression are transparent and inclusive of all activity. It can be more difficult to develop measures of excellence for the recognition of enterprise, but is imperative to ensure parity in status and progression. A report by the NGCE and CIHE supports these findings and recommends that universities

"*make bold changes to reward and remuneration frameworks to recognise the entrepreneurial behaviour of academics and practitioners*".[9]

Students and alumni

A successful enterprise culture extends across a university to actively include its students and alumni, both in establishing the culture and carrying it forward. Whether these activities involve 'Dragon Den-type' competitions, business ideas challenges, or enterprise clubs it is imperative that the enterprise ethos is embedded in the university curriculum, is eligible for the award of university academic credit, enriches the student experience and provides extra-curricular opportunities.

Direct contact with employers and entrepreneurs, together with an exposure to incubation facilities, work placements, internships and volunteering all ensure that students gain confidence in their ability to tackle live commissions and projects, operate in real-world situations and secure experiences that distinguish them in the market place. Research-led teaching enriched by a range of real-life experiences delivers an enterprise-led pedagogic approach.

Business model

To maximise this enterprise culture, a new business model is needed, especially given that enterprise in action relies upon being bold and taking informed risks with ruthless

7   Salter, A. Tartari, V. and D'Este, P. 2010. The Republic of Engagement Exploring UK Academic Attitudes to Collaborating with Industry and Entrepreneurship. August 2010.

8   Perkmann, M and Salter A. Entrepreneurial academics need support. Financial Times. December 20 2010

9   Herrmann, K. Hannon, P. Cox, J. and Ternouth P. 2008. Developing Entrepreneurial Graduates: Putting entrepreneurship at the centre of higher education. CIHE

attention to delivery. Traditional models of operation, university committee structures and upward delegation do not adequately support enterprise given the intrinsic need to be agile. The 2009 PA Consulting report summarised that need for change

"*from an 'old world' of public funding entitlements to a still-forming 'new world' of income earned through value delivered.*"[10]

Universities will need to adapt their business model to embrace these changes and adopt a solutions-orientated mindset - responsive to expressed and anticipated customer needs and demands. The enterprise model places a premium on securing shared solutions through partnership working and a belief that a university can impact positively on the community it serves.

External culture – creating pathways for change

In 2010, the Secretary of State for Business, Innovation and Skills[11] reflected that enterprise in the widest sense, for example social enterprise, is vital in supporting people to

"*become self-motivated entrepreneurs with a clear stake in their communities and what they do*".

Universities, typically though their student body, engage in community volunteering projects, work with schools as part of outreach and liaison, act as supernumerary members of the workforce out on placement and engage in aspects of social enterprise or community engagement.

Enterprise is not simply about the number of spin-off/start-up companies or business contracts; it is about value creation through cultural transformation, innovation and the exploitation of ideas. Enterprise universities create a seamless pathway, at the heart of a national landscape for innovation and creativity - providing a strong and diverse network, creating a critical mass of activity and further developing their anchor status as beacons or 'hubs' of enterprise and as a catalyst for change.

The enterprise ecosystem

While focused on the role of national governments to ignite venture creation and growth, Isenberg[12] discussed the key principles in developing an entrepreneurship

10 Boxall, Mike .2009. Escaping the Red Queen Effect. PA Consulting Group
11 Vince Cable. Keynote speech on Growth, CASS Business School, 3rd June 2010
12 Isenberg, Daniel J. 2010. How to start an entrepreneurial revolution. Harvard Business Review, June 2010

ecosystem. These principles provide a useful checklist for universities interested in establishing and maintaining an enterprise culture:

- Articulate a clear vision of what an enterprise-led approach and ethos looks like for the university.

- Build your bespoke enterprise ecosystem around local conditions and develop to support the local environment.

- Engage the private sector from the start with SMEs playing an important role alongside multinationals and community groups:

   "regional economic growth is highly correlated with the presence of many small, entrepreneurial employers – not a few big ones"[13].

- Establish opportunities for 'quick wins' by building a network of vibrant enterprise change agents.

- Ensure that the university reward structure is transparent and enterprise commands an equal status to teaching and research.

Professor Wendy Purcell *is Vice-Chancellor at the University of Plymouth.*

Caroline Chipperfield *is Policy Advisor to the Vice-Chancellor at the University of Plymouth.*

The University of Plymouth *has a clear mission to be enterprise-led in everything it does and articulates this through its student experience. It is a top 50 UK research university and (in partnership) oversees a network of incubation and innovation spaces across the South West, managing over £100million worth of assets.*

13 Glaeser, E. and Kerr, W. 2010. The Secret to job growth: think small. Harvard Business Review July-August 2010.

Universities at the centre of growth: The role of business-engaged universities

Libby Aston and Sam Jones

> *"A business facing university has a revolving door with business and the professions – not an interface or a portal but true interaction"[1]*

Universities are key to growth. They play a central role to the UK economy and society, growing future talent, research and innovation. The economic and social benefits of our diverse university sector have been well documented over the years as commentators and government have tried to influence the role and shape of the sector. At this moment in time, between Browne and the forthcoming White Paper, we should take the opportunity to reassert the role of universities and their contribution to the future development of our country as we seek to grow out of the recession. We must strengthen our vision for the UK economy, built on knowledge and innovation that is driven by a successful and diverse university sector. It is through this approach that we will be able to fully realise the contribution that universities make, in particular the role of business-engaged universities.

An innovation-driven economy

Innovation and the commercialisation of research are key drivers of growth. Recent research has confirmed that innovation and high-tech approaches are the most likely to be successful in driving economic recovery and economic growth in the UK economy. Innovation was responsible for two-thirds of productivity growth between 2000-2007 and was the common defining feature of the fastest growing 6% of businesses between 2002 -2008. These businesses generated half of all new jobs created during this time.

Human capital, particularly graduate-level skills, is now the primary indicator of future economic growth. The proportion of our working population with graduate-level skills, along with our science and research base, will determine the pattern of our future economic growth and our ability to achieve the innovation-based economy that we are striving for.

If we stand still we will fall behind – our global competitors are continuing to invest heavily in universities despite their own budget deficits. In 2000, the UK was 3rd amongst top industrialised nations in terms of the proportion of young people

1   Professor Tim Wilson (2011) Keeping knowledge at the centre of growth, http://www.university-alliance.ac.uk/Keeping knowledge at the centre of growth A5.pdf [Accessed 15.04.11]

graduating. In 2008 we had fallen to 15th position because our competitor countries have been investing at a faster rate than us.

Universities key to growth

Universities are no longer just a part of the education system; they play a central role in driving economic growth. Many countries are putting universities, innovation and research at the heart of their growth strategies. Obama has declared the USA will "out-innovate" and "out-educate" the world by investing in research and development and calling the private sector to put more money into finding solutions to the global challenges facing society.

The USA is not alone. President Sarkozy is taking France in the opposite direction to the UK by recognising higher education and research as the solution to the recession and bringing forward and consolidating investment in both. In Australia, the Government last year announced a 25% increase to the previous year's budget for science and innovation. In Germany, Chancellor Merkel has announced their goal to create a 'Bildungsrepublik', an educated and learning republic, involving a €12 billion increase in the budget for education and teaching by 2013.

In fact, public investment in our universities is already lower than the OECD average – we are lagging behind countries like Poland and Slovenia as well as the US, Canada, Sweden and Germany. We have to consider carefully the consequences of continuing to move down this ranking in terms of our international competitiveness. We need to ask what is it that these countries and, indeed, most other OECD countries are recognising that we are not? We need to move beyond this debate and establish the central position of universities in our economy. Global companies will not invest in the UK without serious public commitments from this Government about their strategic investment in higher education and research.

A sector to meet the challenges

One of the strengths of our university sector is its diversity. We must recognise that it is a vital, rich ecosystem with different and important areas each playing their part. At University Alliance we are striving to demonstrate the importance of the role business-engaged universities are playing, for the sector, society and the economy.

Universities working in partnership with business makes sense. Not just for the economy but for the future of talent, research and innovation in the UK. Strong links with business are a central focus of Alliance universities. The University Alliance represents twenty-three large universities that work closely with business to deliver world-class research, a high quality student experience and work-ready graduates across the UK. These are universities undertaking world-leading research, often in highly rated STEM departments, working closely with industry to generate near-market solutions and start new businesses.

Our recent report, *21st Century universities: engines of an innovation-driven economy*, found that the most successful approach is one where business engagement is embedded across the university, through everything it does. The aim of Alliance universities is to have a model of knowledge exchange rather than knowledge transfer – business engagement isn't just an add-on at the end of the research process. Rather, it needs to be intricately woven through everything the university does. New ideas and innovation are formed out of this partnership, together driving economic growth.

Alliance universities have strong expertise in this approach. They have developed strong partnerships with both national and international business to actively embed businesses engagement across all they do. This builds collaboration on curriculum design, research delivering solutions, graduates, research and innovation that is relevant to the needs of the economy and society. The results of this approach can be seen in the high proportion of professionally accredited courses they deliver, their high graduate employability levels, world-leading research and the impact they have in the UK and internationally.

To be able to grow and compete in an increasingly globalised innovation-driven knowledge economy, the UK has to put science and innovation at the top of the agenda. We need the public commitment to this focus and to long-term investment. As Lord Sainsbury so aptly put it:

> *"The best way for the UK to make the most of globalisation opportunities is to support the restructuring of British companies into high-value goods, services and industries. We should seek to compete with emerging economies in a 'race to the top' rather than a 'race to bottom'"*[2].

This approach to business engagement is key to economic growth in the UK. With the state of the economy and its fragile growth, we need a clear vision for the future of the economy. We need a vision that recognises that universities are central to the growth strategy and to strengthening the UK's global competitive advantage. We need to send a clear message to our Global competitors and secure the confidence of inward investors and UK Plc by putting into place the pillars for growth and a sustainable future. Without this clarity we risk missing the opportunities to become leaders in the global knowledge and innovation economy that emerges over the years to come.

2 *Lord Sainsbury of Turville (2007) The Race to the Top: A Review of Government's Science and Innovation Policies* http://www.rsc.org/images/sainsbury_review051007_tcm18-103116.pdf

Libby Aston is Director of The University Alliance and has held previous roles at The Russell Group, the Parliamentary Select Committee for Education and Skills, the Higher Education Funding Council for England (HEFCE) and the Higher Education Policy Institute (HEPI).

Sam Jones is Head of Communications and Public Affairs at The University Alliance, with previous roles working for Vince Cable and Peter Mandelson at the Department for Business, Innovation and Skills and in the private sector, including with Harrods.

The University Alliance is a group of 23 major, business-engaged universities committed to delivering world-class research and a quality student experience around the UK.

Universities and The Knowledge Age

David Docherty

University and business relations have always ebbed and flowed. For the most part the relationship has been fruitful, creative and collaborative. On occasion, it's been a dialogue between at best dysfunctional friends, at worst, warring tribes. But post the Browne Review we should take the opportunity for new and broader thinking about the role of universities in a knowledge-based economy.

There are as many definitions of the knowledge economy as there are economists trying to define it. I simply take it as axiomatic that any useful definition will stretch well beyond the creative, digital and information technology industries (CDIT) and encompass manufacturing and services, where ideas are also a major economic driver. This results in the uglier, but more accurate concept of a knowledge-based economy powered by the internet (which is the equivalent of steam for the first industrial revolution, and oil and electricity for the second).

This has profound implications for what universities do in engaging with the economic life of the nation, and raises challenging questions about some taken-for-granted assumptions about business-university collaboration. For example, universities have been consistently lectured about their role in developing the skills agenda. But is 'skill' a knowledge-based concept, or is it a term best left for industries that require rote learning and mechanical responses to repeatable problems? Skills are a necessary, but not remotely sufficient condition of economic and business success.

A knowledge-based economy requires experts who are self-reflective, critical of existing methods, intellectually restless and passionate about doing things better. Experts are the 'cybernauts' of the knowledge age. They are built for the systemic complexity of modern manufacturing, services and creative businesses, for the repeated shocks of the new, and for a future where cannibalising your own market is preferable to becoming someone else's spam in a can.

The race will be won by economies which produce the highest calibre expertise to sit alongside smart money and coherent government policies. Universities have always been there to produce experts – from the earliest degrees in law, rhetoric, religion, astronomy and medicine, to the latest on quantum mechanics and digital media. And how businesses work with universities on anticipating the expertise required for the next wave of global change is of vital importance to their success. We must advance the debate beyond the hackneyed realms of STEM versus non-STEM, hard versus soft skills, oven-ready graduates versus thoughtful citizens.

Language traps as well as enables, and I think there is a strong argument that it is time to refresh the concepts that businesses and universities use to describe their joint challenges. We need a Big Conversation for The Knowledge Age. One that fully represents the complexities of living in modern businesses, and helps shape the thinking of the next generation of experts who will leave higher education knowing that expertise is something they will spend their lives gaining and utilising. A key role of a university is to produce people who have learned how to learn.

The Council for Industry and Higher Education (CIHE) has begun this Big Conversation, with its Task Forces that bring together senior business leaders and Vice Chancellors. The first, *The Fuse*, focussed on the Creative, Digital and IT industries (CDIT for short) and recommended that UK administrations should put the CDIT industries alongside STEM at the heart of their growth strategies, that universities should recognise that CDIT businesses require graduates who can operate simultaneously across multiple technological and creative disciplines (and that this should be recognised in undergraduate education, as it is increasingly in Doctoral courses), and that ICT in schools should be radically overhauled to ensure that universities are receiving the right flow of talent.

The second report, *Powering Up*, focussed on cooperation for success in advanced manufacturing. It argued that universities are vital to advanced manufacturing growth, and should be central to the success of Local Enterprise Partnerships, the Technology Innovation Centres and the Regional Growth Fund. It went on to recommend that the Government and devolved administrations establish Advanced Manufacturing Enterprise Centres (AMECs), which would integrate universities with entrepreneurs, both in SMEs and major businesses, through a range of coherently managed relationships.

Powering Up also recommended that universities be more open with their IP and, indeed, should make as much of it available for free to advanced manufacturing businesses, looking to the Glasgow University model of offering up to 95% of their IP as an example. Finally, the report argued that it was the responsibility of big businesses to work with universities to increase the quality of knowledge and information in smaller businesses in their supply chains.

Success in the knowledge-economy requires integrated thinking of the highest order. Other governments across the globe are forcing the pace through *dirigiste* policies that create and hold knowledge in the country that funds them (China) or through special taxes on, for example, extraction industries (Brazil). The UK cannot and will not pursue that route, looking instead for market-based solutions to these challenges. However, markets on their own will never supply the intellectual capital needed for the volume of innovation required in a modern business. Too few people appreciate that Silicon Valley was built not once but twice by defence department funding via the Defence Advanced Research Projects Agency (DARPA), which spawned industries around both semiconductors and the internet.

Government has a pivotal role in ensuring that the UK can be a major player in a knowledge-based global economy, not least in signalling that it understands the needs of businesses and universities as their relationship continues to develop within it.

David Docherty is <u>Chief Executive of the Council For Industry and Higher Education (CIHE)</u>, and Chairman of the Digital Television Group, which is the industry body for digital television in the UK.

<u>**CIHE**</u> is a strategic leadership network of blue-chip companies working with vice chancellors and universities to develop the UK's knowledge-base economy.

Education, business and government: a new partnership for the 21st Century

Julie Mercer

Education in the UK is undergoing a seismic shift. From changes in policy on SureStart through to higher education, the Coalition Government is reshaping the relationship between individuals and education. Within the context of economic recovery and the work to eliminate the UK's fiscal deficit, the Government is rethinking its core obligations to citizens across a range of public services, including education. A fundamental, challenge is to agree when it is appropriate to pay and when intervention is required to drive best value for the taxpayer, the individual or family, and for the economy. What is the role of government, business and the education system in addressing this? This paper provides an employer's perspective on these issues.

With university fees set to increase in 2012 and the uncertain economic outlook, many potential students are questioning whether university is the right choice for them and thinking about a broader range of options open to them. The changes provoke some 'first-principles' questions: What value will a university education bring me? How much debt will I have and what impact will this have on my future? Will the degree I am planning to study and the university I intend to go to give me the edge I need to be successful in the job market? What alternative options should I consider?

Investing in future generations is a responsibility employers share. We need to find better ways of equipping students with information they need to help them make informed choices. Recent research by Deloitte for the Education & Employers Taskforce confirmed the lack of visibility of employers and good information about career options in many schools.[1] Coupled with a real need to diversify the talent pool within which businesses look for talented young employees, employers must think differently about how they engage with schools and young people.

The further education (FE) system has a strong track record of working with employers to meet their needs. Some of the most innovative are working in partnership with business, jointly investing in the development of the future local workforce, sharing facilities and responsibility for training, and creating a cultural fit between the two organisations that continuously reinforces the links between training, development and the world of work.

---

1   http://www.educationandemployers.org/media/7630/deloitte%20eet%20young%20people%20succeed%20report%20final.pdf

The introduction of University Technical Colleges (UTCs), the expansion of modern apprenticeships and the findings of the recent report by Professor Alison Wolf, all recognise the need for high quality technical and vocational routes to employment. Raising the standing of vocational routes should be a priority for any modern economy where competitive advantage is underpinned by the calibre of technical skills available to attract and retain businesses. Building an entrepreneurial mindset right from the early years and throughout the educational journey should run through the curriculum and educational pedagogy.

To be successful, closer links with business will be critical. Education providers need to be more customer focused and should shape their programmes to reflect what learners and businesses demand. At the same time, businesses must recognise that, to get the most out of their partnerships with educators, they need to share strategic plans and provide each other with the confidence to invest. They should also provide students with well developed work experience and internship opportunities.

So what can businesses do to support schools, colleges and universities in their communities? The responses can be practical and relatively low cost for businesses. For example, providing schools with material and knowledge that mix subject learning with insight, experience and role models from the world of work. This could include information on the how the latest research or technology is being used by industry, information about the types of jobs available, raising aspiration through work placement and entrepreneurial projects, visiting lecturers or tutors on related courses, and mentoring and coaching for students and teachers.

For others, the level of partnership might be greater, including though helping schools, colleges and universities procure or have access to other services such as HR, finance or technology, and making better use of the purchasing power and expertise within businesses.

The Government's policy to encourage free schools and Academies to take control of education outcomes in their locality creates further opportunities for business to engage with education in a practical way. Current policy and the concept of a 'Big Society' offers opportunity for local groups and charities to strengthen their support for schools, colleges and universities. If the ambition to transform most schools into Academies is to be realised, business will need to play a role. They can sponsor schools, provide business services and partner with parent and teacher groups to provide the expertise needed to set up free schools.

Being clear about the benefits businesses and educational institutions gain from working together, in terms of opportunities to enrich learning as well as business service expertise can, with the right incentives and regulatory framework, raise standards and reduce costs. For many organisations making the links with education providers is still challenging. Government needs to simplify the qualification system so that employers and students understand what the qualifications mean. Schools, colleges and universities need to provide better information about the quality of the courses they offer and the opportunities they will open for the learner.

As over 23,000 schools move to Academy status, there is a risk of isolation together with few economies of scale or shared development. But the reality may be somewhat different with existing and new academy providers joining forces to create federations and communities of schools. This could involve strategic partnerships with businesses and the creation of local systems that involve primary and secondary schools, a UTC, FE providers, Sure Start centres and even a university within the local community. This model offers the potential to improve choice and offer alternative learning pathways (academic or technical) to young people throughout their education. It also provides real links and opportunities with local businesses and improved value for money as people, systems and processes are shared across the group.

At Deloitte we have tried to align what we do with our education partners with the strengths and expertise within our own business. Our sponsorship of Teach First means we can work with some of the most disadvantaged schools within our communities and support talented young people in these schools through their studies. Our staff provide coaching and mentoring support to Teach First teachers and to students, encouraging them to aim high and consider university and continued education or training. The *BrightStart Deloitte School Leaver* programme, offers a new alternative pathway for joining Deloitte and gaining qualifications, in addition to the traditional higher education route.[2]

As important as technical or academic capabilities are the 'soft skills' that can be used within the workplace. Examples of 'soft skills' are working as part of a team, being able to communicate with others, managing and motivating teams, and being able to interact with people outside of your direct team. Gaining work experience or simply being a member of a club at school or university can all help to develop these skills before they are needed for employment.

Our award-winning *Deloitte Employability Programme* provides over 40,000 young people with a Level 2 Qualification through a network of Deloitte Employability Centres located in further education colleges and universities across the UK.[3] This

2   http://careers.deloitte.com/united-kingdom/students/students_undergraduates.aspx?CountryContentID=16628

3   http://www.deloitte.com/view/en_GB/uk/about/community-investment/skills-and-education/employability-skills/index.htm

qualification, developed in collaboration with Edexcel and with investment from Deloitte over the past 4 years of over £2m, arose in direct response to our clients highlighting the challenges of finding employment-ready school leavers and graduates. The results have been astounding with 89% of graduates going on to full-time employment or full-time study at a higher level than the previous six months after completing the course.

Julie Mercer is a Partner in Deloitte's consulting practice and leads the education services practice.

Deloitte *is a major professional services provider and has around 12,000 partners and staff in the UK. In the United Kingdom, Deloitte works with a majority of the FTSE 100 and many branches of government. Our advisory work spans audit, accountancy, tax, corporate finance and consulting. Deloitte LLP is the United Kingdom member firm for Deloitte Touche Tohmatsu Limited, a UK private company limited by guarantee.*

Section eight – Are there global lessons to learn?

The future of university rankings

Phil Baty

Let us be frank. University rankings are crude. They simply cannot capture – let alone accurately measure – many of the things that matter most in higher education: how a great lecturer can transform the lives of their students for example, or how much free enquiry enhances our society. They can never be objective, because their indicators and methodologies are based on the subjective judgment of the compilers. At their worst, university rankings can impose uniformity on a sector that thrives on diversity. They can pervert university missions and distract policymakers. When they are done badly, they can be manipulated for unfair gain. They can mislead the public.

I admit all of this even though I am myself a 'ranker'. Indeed, I am the Editor of the world's most widely-cited (and perhaps most controversial) global university ranking system – The Times Higher Education World University Rankings – and I am proud of what I do. Why? Because I believe that as long as rankers are responsible and transparent, university rankings can be a positive force in higher education.

Rankings can help us understand and find a way through the dramatic changes we are facing. Speaking at the World 100 Reputation Network conference at the University of Hong Kong last year, Peter Upton the Director of British Council, Hong Kong said:

> *"We are living through one of those tipping points where in five years, [commentators will say] that this was the period when the landscape changed for ever, when the speed of reputational growth and decline suddenly accelerated.*
>
> *We all accept that higher education is borderless - ideas know no boundaries, do not accord any significance to geography and maps - and that is equally true of reputations and university rankings."*

The facts of rapid internationalisation are clear: 3.3 million students now study outside their home country; UK institutions have 162 satellite campuses on overseas soil; almost half of all UK research papers are now written with a co-author from overseas. We are in a world of global education hubs, of joint degrees, faculty and student mobility schemes, franchised programmes, global research networks and bi-national universities.

We are also entering a world of mass higher education, with new forms of delivery and new providers of higher education, changing the traditional world order. But there is an information gap, with a growing need for clear – and yes, easily accessible – comparative information for all stakeholders. National governments need information when they are investing billions into universities to drive the knowledge-based sectors of the economy. Industry needs help in looking where to invest R&D money and where to find the top talent. Higher education leaders need to understand the shifting global sands and to improve strategy and performance. Newly emerging institutions, often in developing countries, need help in clearly demonstrating their excellence to the world, against better known and more established brands. Faculty, seeking to foster new research partnerships and consider career options, need help in identifying new opportunities. And perhaps most importantly, in a global market, students and their parents looking to make the right choice of degree course, wherever in the world it might be delivered, need help. This is crucial as the world gets smaller, global demand for higher education gets bigger, and choices become more bewildering.

Here to stay

As long as those who compile them are responsible and transparent, rankings have a positive role to play. Make no mistake, rankings are here to stay. Ellen Hazelkorn of the Dublin Institute of Technology, has cataloged the extraordinary growth and influence of rankings in her new book Rankings and the Battle for World-Class Excellence: How Rankings are re-shaping higher education. She writes:

> *"There is a growing obsession with university rankings around the world. What started as an academic exercise in the early 20th Century in the US became a commercial 'information' service for students in the 1980s and the progenitor of a 'reputation race' with geo-political implications today… rankings are transforming and reshaping higher education."*

From influencing immigration policies to prompting multi-billion pound national policies, she has demonstrated clearly how much rankings are shaping behaviour.

So given their increasing importance, surely the best way forward is for rankers to work closely with the university community and engage openly with their critics, to ensure they offer tables that are meaningful, with all the necessary caveats and health warnings. Who better to do that than Times Higher Education (THE) magazine? THE has been serving the higher education world for forty years – it is our anniversary this year. Through our website, and a new digital edition available from the beginning of this year as an iPhone and iPad application, we are reaching an ever-growing global audience which now amounts to more than 100,000 readers a week. We live or die by our reputation among university staff and policymakers as a trusted source of news, analysis and data week in and week out. Our rankings are part of that. They need to stand up to the close scrutiny of our highly intelligent and demanding readers. That is why in late 2009 we brought in one of the world's most trusted and respected information specialists, Thomson Reuters, to work with us to develop an entirely new methodology, and to collect and supply all our world rankings data for the future. That is why we published our entirely new rankings system in September 2010 only after ten months of open consultation and frank self-criticism, and after detailed expert advice from more than 50 advisors across 15 countries.

The new *Times Higher Education* <u>World University Rankings</u>, used 13 indicators to cover the university's three core missions: research, knowledge transfer and teaching. With the proliferation of different ranking systems by different ranking agencies, all with different agendas, Times Higher Education's unique selling points are responsibility, transparency and, most importantly given our audience, academic rigour.

For the 2010-11 rankings, we made major improvements to our reputation survey by using the invited views of more than 13,000 targeted, identifiable and experienced academics, questioned on their narrow fields of expertise. We employed a bibliometric indicator that drew on more than 25 million citations from five million journal articles over five years. And we fully normalised the citations data to take account of major variations in citations behaviour between subjects. We made the first serious attempt to capture the teaching and learning environment through five separate indicators – an essential element of any university, but one missed by the other world-ranking systems. They are new rankings, more appropriate for a new era.

The future

One of the things I am most proud of is that we have handed much of the rankings data over to the user. We have created a rankings application for the iPhone and iPad, which I believe represents a major step forward in the field.

Of course, we choose our indicators and weightings very carefully and only after lengthy consultation. But with the app, the weightings can be changed by the user to suit their individual needs. If you don't agree with our weightings, you can set your own. Such transparency and interactivity with the user is more responsible and I personally believe it is the future of world rankings.

In an article in Times Higher Education last year, Ben Wildavsky, author of the Great Brain Race: How Global Universities are Reshaping the World, said:

> *"We now have a global academic marketplace. It seems to me that education markets, like other kinds of market, need information to function effectively. We're also living in the age of accountability, so rankings aren't going away."*

I would go a step further. Rankings are certainly not going to go away, and as long as those who rank invest properly in serious research and sound data, as long as they are frank about the limitations of the proxies they employ, as long as they help to educate the users with clear health warnings and keep discussing improvements – rankings are going to become an essential and valued tool in helping to guide us through times of unprecedented change and uncertainty in global higher education.

Phil Baty *is Editor of the Times Higher Education* World University Rankings *and Deputy Editor of the Times Higher Education magazine. The latest world university rankings results can be found here:* http://bit.ly/thewur.

Times Higher Education *is the world's most authoritative source of information about higher education. Designed specifically for professional people working in higher education and research, Times Higher Education was founded in 1971 and has been online since 1995.*

A different horizon: higher education in South Africa

Fathima Dada

The latest available statistics from Higher Education South Africa (HESA) demonstrate that currently around 500,000 students are enrolled on a full-time basis at academic institutions across South Africa. This includes full universities, comprehensive universities and universities of technology. Statistics from 2001 and 2009 respectively show a cumulative increase in enrolment, across these institutions, of around 140,000 (35 per cent), from a figure of 401,000 in 2001 to 541,000 in 2009. This figure does not include the Further Education and Training Colleges (FET), where another c.125,000 students are currently enrolled across the country. The Department of Education in South Africa is aiming to increase this figure to a million by 2015.

Annually about 500,00 pupils leave the final year of schooling ('Matric'), of which around 50 to 60 per cent may achieve university exemption, resulting in about 60,000 making it into Higher Institution's of Learning. The remainder either enter the FET colleges, look for employment, become self-employed or join the long queue of the unemployed, of which there are estimated to be c.8m currently.

The Department of Education is now in the process of announcing a newly revised educational structure which includes an Adult Matric. This addition to the educational landscape is meant to capture those many adult individuals who never managed to obtain a final school leavers' qualification.

South Africa's academic institutions are under pressure to fulfil the economic requirements of a growing economy, helping to produce a labour force that will be able to meet the needs of South Africa, the African Nation and the wider global economy. Pressure is being put upon academic institutions to address the skills shortages experienced by both government and business, especially in the Sciences, Engineering and Mathematics. While there is an over-supply of business graduates leaving the universities, there is a shortfall in Nursing, Health Care and Medicine.

Bursaries and scholarships are increasingly being made available to promising students, offering them entry into these fields, yet still the number of graduates does not meet the requirements of the economy. Furthermore, there is a paucity of graduates moving on into academia and research.

A few years ago, South African academic institutions were encouraged to cap their enrolment figures and focus on ensuring that students pass the course that they register for, within the minimum amount of time. This presents a huge cost issue for institutions. At FET colleges the pass-rate has been lower than 10 per cent in recent years, while some universities have an average pass rate of only 50%.

Some of the reasons behind these high failure rates are a lack of preparedness for academic life, a poor educational background, lack of support at academic institutions, financial pressures, and lack of knowledge about how to study.

At some institutions students require six years to pass a three year degree, costing the institution – and the country – a great deal of money. A variety of institutions offer measures to address these issues: support for students via extensive tutoring structures, flexible study programs, and different entry/exit levels for programs. Some institutions, notably the distance learning institutions, offer study guides to students that enable self-learning. Often these study guides are meant to be additional resources, on top of prescribed textbooks, but sometimes they replace textbooks altogether.

Few institutions make these textbooks compulsory however, as many fear to be seen adding additional costs to already costly fee-structures and financially burdened students. There is some proof, at some institutions such as the Mangusutho University of Technology in Durban, that adding the cost of a textbook to the study-fee of the student, thus making the book immediately available to the student, has dramatically increased pass-rates. However few institutions have decided to follow this example.

Curriculum reviews are currently happening in a variety of fields – namely Nursing, Teacher Education and the various Business/Commerce disciplines – in order to address national requirements better. For example the revised Nursing curriculum is meant to address the lack of nurses overall, but also issues like there being too few nurses who fulfil basic nursing duties, too few nurses who manage to move from a diploma to a degree course, and too few nurses who do research and become Doctoral students.

So, what does this complex web of data say about Higher Education in South Africa?

Firstly, it paints a dynamic picture of a sector that is very active and responsive to national needs. To accommodate these needs, a growing private HE and FE sector is merging. Also, the high cost of university education (compared to Europe) has encouraged parents and students to demand better quality and throughput of HE institutions. And finally, for the first time since democracy in 1994, the Rainbow Nation has started addressing the need to grow a cadre of young South Africans ready to be leaders in the national, continental and global economy.

Fathima Dada is the CEO of Pearson Southern Africa. She has worked on educational policies for the Ministry of Education for the past 11 years, and continues to do this and community development work, especially in rural areas of South Africa.

Pearson Southern Africa (PSA) can trace its roots back to 1893 when the company Maskew Miller was founded in South Africa. The company merged with Longman South Africa almost 100 years later to form Maskew Miller Longman and then with Heinemann South Africa in 2010. PSA today is the largest and most successful educational publisher in Africa and publishes in over 50 languages.

Blue skies: new thinking about the future of higher education

Higher education in the UK, and beyond, appears to be experiencing a period of unprecedented change. Together, global trends and national policies are generating a debate that is increasingly focussed on the cost of higher education. Tuition fees, research grants and ROI are the issues of the day.

It's time to widen the debate. The Pearson Centre for Policy and Learning is pleased to present a range of bold, new ideas about the future of higher education. Leading experts, including a few less-well known voices, set out their vision for the future.

There is disagreement at times about priorities, but together this diverse collection demonstrates the qualities of higher education and how it can drive both economic growth and better wellbeing in the future.

Pearson Centre for Policy and Learning   IPN: 978-0-997-86378-9
One90 High Holborn   www.pearsonblueskies.com
London
WC1V 7BH
+44 (0)20 7190 4330